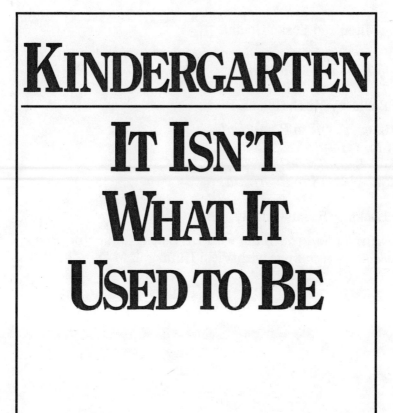

KINDERGARTEN

IT ISN'T WHAT IT USED TO BE

KINDERGARTEN

IT ISN'T WHAT IT USED TO BE

GETTING YOUR CHILD READY FOR THE POSITIVE EXPERIENCE OF EDUCATION

Susan Golant and Mitch Golant, Ph.D.

LOWELL HOUSE

Los Angeles

Contemporary Books

Chicago

Library of Congress Cataloging-in-Publication Data

Golant, Susan K.
    Kindergarten—It isn't what it used to be: getting your child ready for the
    positive experience of education/Susan Golant and Mitch Golant.
        p.   cm.
    ISBN 0-929923-14-6
    1. Readiness for school. 2. Kindergarten. I. Golant, Mitch.
    II. Title.
    LB1132.G65 1990
    372.21'8—dc20   89-13531
                                                                          CIP

The authors would like to thank the following publisher for permission to reprint:
From the book, *Annabelle Swift, Kindergartner* by Amy Schwartz. Text and
illustrations copyright © 1988 by Amy Schwartz. Reprinted with permission of
the publisher, Orchard Books.

Lowell House
1875 Century Park East, Suite 220
Los Angeles, CA 90067

Publisher: JACK ARTENSTEIN
Vice President/Editor-in-Chief: JANICE GALLAGHER
Marketing Manager: ELIZABETH WOOD
Design: MIKE YAZZOLINO

Manufactured in the United States of America
10   9   8   7   6   5   4   3   2   1

To parents and teachers who every day, in little ways, dedicate their lives to what's best for children.

ACKNOWLEDGEMENTS

We are deeply indebted to many dedicated professionals who helped us in the shaping of this book. Teacher Arla Capps, child developmentalist Judy Steingieser, and nursery school director Jane Zuckerman gave generously of their time and expertise. Friends and colleagues Dr. Anne Panofsky, Dr. Helana Barry, Dr. Luba Fischer, Dr. Nan Krakow, and Renee Schwartz, L.C.S.W., offered advice and useful points of reference. We would also like to express our appreciation to the National Association for the Education of Young Children for their prompt response to our queries and to our editor at Lowell House, Janice Gallagher, for her careful reading and many useful suggestions.

Most of all, we would like to express our gratitude to our children for allowing us to mine their childhoods for material. Without them, our writing parenting books would be inconceivable.

CONTENTS

PART 1

WHAT KINDERGARTEN READINESS REALLY MEANS

CHAPTER 1

Kindergarten Ain't What
It Used to Be

When we decided to write *Kindergarten—It Isn't What It Used to Be,* both of us were excited by the prospect of helping parents of preschoolers with what we saw as an important life transition. As we discussed the concept of this book with our publisher and editor, we conceived of a reassuring, warm, and funny volume that would offer advice based on our family's adventures and foibles, much as our last joint endeavor, a book on disciplining preschoolers, had done.

After all, we thought, we have had lots of parenting experience—our daughters Cherie and Aimee have successfully moved on beyond kindergarten to high school and college. Mitch is a former educator and a clinical psychologist with a busy family practice that includes many young children. Susan is a journalist and author of articles and books on parenting and women's issues. Both of us had already written several books for parents in collaboration with others and also with one another. What's more, we are still in our early 40s—close enough in age to today's parents of preschoolers to be able to relate to their concerns.

"Sure," we said. "Getting children ready for kindergarten? We can cover that topic easily."

We were wrong. What began as a simple tried-and-true how-to book has turned into a much more complex evaluation of the issues that parents are facing today as their children advance toward the big event—the start of elementary school. We're here to tell you that your questions and concerns are valid and not to be resolved with a formula or a pat answer.

But we jump ahead. Let's go back to that moment of shock when we concluded that kindergarten readiness was not the simple issue we had imagined it to be. We discovered that in recent years this subject has become a political hot potato. Our book would have to be more than a gentle discussion of useful tips for parents to prepare themselves and their children emotionally. Unless we addressed the real concerns, we were going to get nowhere fast.

We decided to seek the help of those fighting it out in the kindergarten trenches. As we became more involved in our research—as we spoke with early-childhood educators, kindergarten teachers, parents, and child developmentalists, as we read books and articles on kindergarten readiness—we came to the realization that kindergarten in the 1990s is nothing like what we (and probably you) experienced in the 1950s and '60s. In fact, it only remotely resembles our daughters' classrooms of 10 and 15 years ago. The basic concept of kindergarten has changed . . . and therein lies the problem.

THE TRICKLE-DOWN PHENOMENON

Walk into a kindergarten classroom today and you'll see more than a pile of wooden blocks or a dress-up corner, a play kitchen or an easel beckoning with blank paper and bright paints. You may be more likely to observe a sea of five-year-old heads bent over paper-and-pencil work—ditto sheets, workbooks, and the like.

"What's going on here?" you may wonder. "Why aren't these kids playing and having fun?"

Good question. Rosalind Charlesworth, professor of curriculum and instruction in the College of Education at Louisiana State University, describes the evolution of kindergarten: "Kindergarten was originally a year of relatively informal education designed to form a bridge from home to more formal schooling in the elementary grades. . . . During the '80's . . . rather than serving a readiness function in the sense of socializing children for future schooling, kindergarten has become an experience for which children need to be ready when they arrive."

In other words, kindergarten used to be the place where children prepared for elementary school. Now, more often than not, it has become a place for which children must prepare in advance. Kindergarten *has become* elementary school.

Developmentalists and early-childhood educators alike decry the fact that the first-grade curriculum has been inappropriately "pushed down" into the kindergarten classroom. The unrealistic expectations and pressures of this new curriculum have doomed some five-year-olds to an intolerable situation of "kindergarten failure." Imagine the damage to a child's emergent ego and his future motivation after he has been labeled a school failure at the tender age of five!

Dr. David Elkind, professor of child study at Tufts University and a leading child-advocate, is highly critical of the current state of kindergarten affairs. He makes his case in *The Hurried Child: Growing Up Too Fast Too Soon:*

> Today there are tax-supported kindergartens in every state, and some twenty-three states are considering programs for four-year-olds. In too many schools kindergartens have now become "one-size-smaller" first grades, and children are tested, taught with workbooks, given homework, and take home a report card. The result of this educational hurrying is that from 10 to 20 percent of kindergarten children are being "retained" or put in "transition" classes to prepare them for the academic rigors of first grade!

The National Association for the Education of Young Children, the nation's largest professional organization of early-childhood educators and child developmentalists, points out why teaching first-grade material in kindergarten is inappropriate in its monograph, *Kindergarten Policy: What Is Best for Children?*

> A great deal of quite conclusive research over half a century tells us that kindergarten-aged children still think like younger children; they think differently, see the world differently, act differently, and have different skills than children of 7 or 8. . . . The kindergarten year is one more important year in a child's lengthy process of growing up. It is not developmentally helpful, or in the long run a success, to push and rush children through it.

HOW HAVE WE GOTTEN INTO THIS MESS?

The many factors contributing to the shift in kindergarten policy seem to have arisen from the social and educational movements of the last 30 years. To begin with, it's important to recognize that fads in education swing like a pendulum from one generation to the next. From the three Rs of our parents' times we have shifted to the "progressive" education of the '50s and then, boosted by Sputnik, to the academic educational reform of the '60s that spawned the "relevance" and creativity of the '70s, and then back again to the basics and accountability of the '80s—the era of limits.

According to the National Association for the Education of Young Children, since the second half of the nineteenth century, "kindergarten programs have been susceptible to the winds of change as society's expectations for education have shifted." The current heightening of expectations arose in part from the social flux that occurred in the '60s and '70s. With more divorce, more working mothers, more single heads of households, and more day-care centers, parents seem to need to see their children as maturing more quickly than they actually do—as being, in Dr. Elkind's words, "competent."

In addition, the Head Start programs developed as part of President Lyndon Johnson's War on Poverty have contributed to the controversy. These programs have been successful in helping socioeconomically disadvantaged youngsters obtain much-needed medical attention and enriching stimulation that is often lacking in their home environments. These programs do help prepare disadvantaged children for school.

When the principles of the Head Start programs are applied to middle-class youngsters, on the other hand, the results can be less satisfactory. Middle-class children don't need the added stimulation; they already have all that's required in their natural environment. To paraphrase one researcher, when you give an emaciated, starving child rich and nutritious food you are helping him, but if you give a child of normal weight rich food, you may be creating a weight problem. Too much of a good thing is not necessarily good.

Kindergarten has even become the subject of international political pressure. Like us, you were probably in school during the post-Sputnik press for better education that occurred in the late '50s and '60s. Today's children also face worldwide competition, but not from the Russians. The standard is now the superior Japanese educational system. According to the National Association for the Education of Young Children, "Currently, our culture of accountability is putting great pressure on principals and teachers in general, and on primary teachers in particular, which in turn puts great pressure on kindergarten teachers"—and, as you can imagine, on preschool teachers and children, as well.

THE PARENTAL DILEMMA

As we see it, you and your preschooler may be caught in the crossfire between the educators and politicos on one side who are taking the childhood out of kindergarten, and the child developmentalists on the other who are screaming that educators are acting to the detriment of young children by stressing academics so early.

What are you to do? You have to deal with school as it exists today, with kindergarten that has been largely integrated into the elementary school curriculum. Should you, then, prepare Sarah with early academics in preschool? Should you put pressure on her? It might seem like the logical choice. But, as we'll explain in greater depth in the chapters to come, that choice is not developmentally appropriate.

A recent article in *The APA Monitor* (the monthly newsletter of the American Psychological Association), entitled "Pushing Preschoolers Doesn't Help, May Hurt," describes a two-year study that looked at more than 200 children and their mothers in 22 schools in Pennsylvania, Delaware, and Vermont. According to the article, "Children of mothers with extremely high expectations tended to be less creative, have more test anxiety, and by first grade, to have no academic advantage over peers whose mothers felt that 'kids should be kids.' "

These results seem to indicate that preschoolers don't benefit from early exposure to academics. At worst, the study could be interpreted to mean that early pressure can hurt children by undermining their good feelings about school.

The article was careful to point out, however, that the findings do not mean that mothers should not have high expectations for their children. In another long-term study researchers found that children whose mothers had high expectations did better than those whose mothers did not. The problem occurs when parental expectations are coupled with negative attitudes such as pushiness, criticalness, rigidity, anxiety, overprotectiveness, domination, perfectionism, and lack of affection.

Your other choice, therefore, is to allow Sarah to be a child for as long as she can. While the developmentalists may applaud that decision (we along with them), unfortunately it doesn't fully deal with the reality before you. You're bound to feel pressure from other parents in the "readiness game," even if you believe that early academics don't help and may in fact be detrimental. Understandably, you don't want Sarah to be left in the academic dust. You must deal with the system as it is, not as you wish it to be.

HOW WE CAN HELP YOU

As we have stated earlier, your concerns about kindergarten readiness are real, and we have no magical answers that will resolve them for you painlessly. Indeed, we wouldn't presume to advise you specifically on what to do with your child. Your preschooler and your family situation are unique, and you will need to make each decision within your own, very personal context. Ultimately, only you can know what is best for your family.

However, we can help you by exploring the issues and by answering questions so that you understand the markers and roadblocks along the way. With foreknowledge, you can make informed decisions rather than panicked last-minute choices between rocks and hard places.

In Chapter 2 we ask the deceptively simple question, *What is kindergarten readiness, anyway?* Of course, the answer is not so simple. It seems that no two people have the same opinion on that score. "Readiness" standards can range from Josh's ability to tie his shoe, to his reciting and writing the alphabet and counting to 30, to his just being five years old. We will also discuss the birthdate factor, which can have great impact on the younger members of a kindergarten class, especially younger boys.

In Chapter 3, we cover the all-important and controversial questions of developmental and readiness testing as indicators of readiness. First we stress the importance of physiological testing to rule out any physical problems that may interfere with the educational process. Then we look at various developmental and readiness tests and explain why developmentalists are up in arms about using these instruments as the sole means of judging whether a preschooler is ready for kindergarten.

Chapter 4 discusses what we feel is the first R of kindergarten education—developing relationships. We stress socialization early on because preschoolers and kindergarteners learn best while interacting with others. Too early and heavy an emphasis on individual-at-the-desk academics can potentially reduce your child's later achievement by eliminating appropriate playtime.

We also give advice about what to look for in your child's behavior to determine if he is becoming appropriately socialized, and we suggest important factors that can promote positive relationships in your child's preschool and kindergarten experience. Finally we discuss how to handle your child if he seems overly aggressive or unusually shy.

In Chapter 5, we explore in greater depth the dangers of hurrying your child academically. We cover the ins and outs of early reading (we had one early reader in our house and one later reader) and how to encourage a lifelong enthusiasm for reading.

Chapter 6 covers our favorite topics in terms of kindergarten readiness. Here we give pointers on how to encourage your child's curiosity, conversation, and creativity, the keys to her future love of learning and her development as a whole child. In truth the academic skills she may pick up during her preschool years pale in comparison to the importance of a sharpened curiosity, the ability to express ideas, and a sense of exploration and creativity. We also discuss the effects of television as it thwarts your child's growth and how you can use TV effectively to encourage conversation and curiosity.

Chapter 7 marks the beginning of Part 2, in which we cover the nuts and bolts of kindergarten more specifically. In this chapter, we discuss what to look for in a kindergarten, whether or not you have a choice as to the school your child will be attending. We also suggest ways you can become involved in the school in order to help the institution and also in an effort to see that your child's needs are met more sensitively. We close the chapter with a discussion of what to look for in after-school care.

This leads logically into Chapter 8: the school visit. We take you through the daily routines of kindergarten step-by-step so that you can guide your preschooler during an observation visit. The more your child familiarizes himself with kindergarten ahead of time, the more secure he will feel once school begins.

In Chapter 9, we cover what to look for in a kindergarten teacher. In our opinion, the ideal teacher loves children and is aware of their individual differences. She uses an integrated approach that takes into account the whole child. She is warm, flexible, and open, yet she has a strong grasp of what needs to be taught and how best to approach her varied classroom. She is a person whom her students can trust and with whom they can have fun. We also discuss what *not* to expect from the classroom teacher, as well as what falls into the domain of your responsibility as parents.

(By the way, because of the preponderance of women in the field of early-childhood education, we will refer to the kindergarten teacher as "she" throughout the book. This is in no way meant to slight the many fine and dedicated men who also work with young children. We use the feminine pronoun only to alleviate stylistic problems.)

In Chapter 10, we help you deal with your kindergartener's school-induced stress as well as life-induced stress and discuss how distress in one area may impact the other. We provide lists of typical stressors for children and give you clues to determine whether your child is experiencing stress. We suggest visualization and relaxation exercises that you can use to relieve some of your child's distress.

Finally, in Chapter 11, we cover how to prepare for the first day of school. We believe that in preparing your preschooler, you also must prepare yourself. The first day of kindergarten is a time of anxiety and mixed feelings for parents and children alike. We suggest ways to address your five-year-old's fears and explore how you can make the transition a positive experience. We cover the pros and cons of staying in class with your child that first day, especially if he cries. We conclude with a discussion of how preparation for kindergarten can also be seen as preparation for life.

Interestingly, when we first drew up an outline for this book, we included a chapter on "What Your Child Should Know" by the time she reaches kindergarten. After much thought and debate, we decided to scratch that idea. We felt that it would convey the wrong message to you and in effect would undermine everything else we were trying to say. In preparing your child for kindergarten, you should consider *who she is* and not try to fit her into some preconceived image of who she *should be* or where she should rank on some scale.

In preparing your child for kindergarten you must consider the person you are dealing with and her welfare. What are her needs? What are her aptitudes and interests? Where is she emotionally, physically, socially, and developmentally? Does she have any areas of expertise or any deficits? How can you best serve her educational needs and help to create a lifelong love and a zest for learning? All other concerns are secondary.

CHAPTER 2

What Is Kindergarten Readiness, Anyway?

These days, kindergarten readiness is a hot and controversial topic. Not so when we were kids. In those days, the best way to get ready for kindergarten was to turn five years old by a given date. It was as simple as that. According to Rosalind Charlesworth, professor of curriculum and instruction at Louisiana State College, "Readiness for elementary education was defined in terms of attitude and motivation rather than specific academic achievements."

The kindergarten accepted all students of a certain age regardless of their stage of maturation, and the teacher designed the program to suit whoever was in the room. It was her responsibility to match the curriculum to her students' needs.

Today, more often than not, the program is established first, according to guidelines for which the teacher is held accountable. Now the burden rests on the child. Can he fit into the program as it exists? Will he be ready? If he's not, what's to be done about it?

THE MANY FACES OF READINESS

As we mentioned in the previous chapter, today there are many criteria for "readiness." Depending on whom you talk to, you will get differing answers about what kindergarten readiness really is. These criteria can include academic factors, such as:

★ Performance on readiness and developmental tests. (We will explore these in greater detail in Chapter 3.)

★ The ability to recite the alphabet and recognize and write random upper- and lowercase letters.

★ The ability to identify the first sound of a word or tell when words rhyme.

★ The ability to write one's name.

★ The ability to count to 20 and recognize numerals.

★ The ability to recite the days of the week and months of the year and to state one's birthday.

★ The ability to draw a person with recognizable features.

★ The ability to name and draw simple geometric shapes like circles, squares, and triangles.

When most parents think of readiness, they automatically turn to these sorts of academic skills. That makes sense because these skills are clearly quantifiable: Can my five-year-old count or give his address and phone number? Does he know the alphabet? Can he spell and write his name? Is he already beginning to read? Does he know an ankle from a wrist? The answers to these questions indicate concrete achievements that you can recognize with relative ease.

However, academics are one component of readiness but not the whole story—far from it. In fact, in our talks with other experts and parents, we have come to believe that readiness doesn't necessarily mean mastery of such skills at all. Developmentalists remind us that when we talk about kindergarten readiness, we must think about the whole child and not just the one facet that seems most obvious.

Most developmentalists with whom we have spoken or whose research we have read state adamantly and reiterate endlessly that in terms of readiness, it matters very little what skills a preschooler has acquired. They stick to the old dictum that a child is ready for kindergarten when she turns five, and it's up to the teacher to make adjustments. As Dr. Charlesworth puts it, "What does 'not ready' mean? Isn't it our job [as teachers] to help each child progress from wherever he or she is?"

To illustrate how academics can be misleading, we'd like to share the experience of a friend of ours. Nancy's November-born son, Brian, had attended an exclusive preschool-to-the-stars in Los Angeles where he had been taught how to read. When he entered kindergarten as one of the youngest in the class, Nancy felt at ease because she knew that Brian was able to handle books. Unfortunately, however, he was lost in just about every other way. He had a hard time following directions, he couldn't sustain his attention, and he wouldn't sit still. Brian has had trouble with school ever since.

Readiness doesn't mean academics exclusively. We would rather take a broader view. From what we have gleaned, we have come to understand that readiness is the setting in place of certain basic building blocks of learning. All kids share in these essentials to varying degrees:

★ Interest in the world around them
★ Curiosity about what's new and different
★ Communication of feelings and ideas
★ Spontaneity in facing life's challenges
★ Flexible thinking and receptivity to new concepts
★ Memory of the past and the ability to apply it to new situations
★ Ability to retain new information
★ Attention span to sustain a complex project
★ Positive self-esteem

How does your child look at the world? Is it a mysterious place full of excitement and wonder? Does she experience joy in watching a butterfly emerge from its cocoon or in finding a robin's nest with newly hatched fledglings? Can she spend 20 minutes watching a spider spin its web or a colony of ants busily scurrying in and out of its home? Does she talk about her new discoveries? Does she find excitement in hearing a new story or making a new friend? These are all elements of readiness.

One child developmentalist with whom we spoke, Judy Steingieser, child-life coordinator at Kaiser-Permanente Hospital in Woodland Hills, California, stressed the importance of self-esteem as a criterion for success in kindergarten. "I would want to know," she said, "how a child feels about himself and shows his feelings. Does the preschooler show joy in relation to objects or other people? Does he feel good about how his body moves in space? Is he able to make his needs known? If he's anxious, that can get in the way. He won't be able to focus if he's worried about where his parents are or who is going to pick him up after school."

SOME SIGNPOSTS OF MATURATION

In an article entitled "Readiness for Kindergarten," Erna Furman, child psychoanalyst and faculty member at Case Western Reserve University School of Medicine, enumerates what she feels to be the most important indicators. We found her list to be very helpful in understanding the broader scope of readiness. When taken together, Ms. Furman's seven maturational issues comprise a backdrop against which other readiness criteria such as academic skills can be measured, giving a better picture of the whole child. They include the child's ability to:

1. Deal with new situations
2. Take care of his bodily needs
3. Form an appropriate relationship with his teacher
4. Form relationships with classmates
5. Play
6. Exert internal controls
7. Recognize, verbalize, and tolerate feelings

Before we look at these one by one, it's important to note that if on some intuitive level you feel your child has any physiological or developmental problem, by all means follow your instincts and check out your suspicions with your pediatrician and a child development specialist. Don't be afraid to seek second or third opinions. If, after sufficient consultation, you feel reassured that the issue is merely maturational, you should understand that patience is the best approach.

Many of Ms. Furman's readiness factors involve such maturational issues. By that we mean neither you nor your child has any control over how quickly the issues resolve themselves. Each child has her own inner clock that governs when she is capable of achieving certain goals. You can think of it in terms of the eruption of teeth, for example, or the onset of puberty. Some kids are early bloomers while others take their own sweet time. Neither pace is better or worse, and there's not much anyone can do about it in either case.

As we examine these indicators, then, think of them as markers on the road to readiness. As you read, try not to make the judgment that if your child can do a certain thing she's "good" and if she can't she's "bad." That's simply not the case. Just as you wouldn't criticize a seedling for not yet being a tree, you should guard against thinking less of your child if she hasn't grown yet in a particular area.

We will also suggest, where appropriate, ways in which your and/or the preschool teacher's positive involvement can support and encourage growth. While you can't hurry things along, there's no point in denying the seedling water and fertilizer!

Ability to Deal with New Situations

When Ethan neared the kindergarten experience, he began to show unending curiosity about the impending event. He asked hundreds of questions about what it would be like; he nagged his parents to drive by the school so that he could see it; he anticipated subjects that he would learn about and the children he would meet.

Once school began, Ethan talked at length about how kindergarten differed from his preschool: There was no nap time. His jacket went into a wardrobe instead of a cubby. He liked playing on the kindergarten yard but he didn't understand why there was no sandbox for his toy trucks. In no time at all, he understood where the kids had to line up for recess and how the milk and cookies were distributed during snack time.

Jennifer, on the other hand, showed little interest in kindergarten, even when her parents tried to engage her in conversation about it. She didn't ask to be taken to see the school and she didn't voice any concerns or anxieties. Once school started, she was slow to get the hang of the daily routine. Most of the time she wandered around the classroom like a bewildered space cadet, not knowing which door led to the bathroom and which to the outside hallway—no matter how many times her teacher told her.

Rather than facing her new situation, as Ethan did, Jennifer panicked at the transition from preschool to kindergarten. She had a hard time integrating her new surroundings and dealing with new situations. She felt lost and confused.

Your preschooler's ability to come to terms with new experiences is an important part of her readiness for kindergarten. According to Ms. Furman, bewildered children face new situations "without inner preparation and cannot bring their knowledge of the familiar to bear on it. Each new piece of learning disorients and overwhelms them because they have to start from scratch."

What's to be done about this? Nothing, necessarily. Difficulty with new situations may simply be a question of maturation. With time, the problem takes care of itself and there may not be much you can do to speed the process along. In fact, that's one of our irritations with the notion of "readiness." Parents may make the mistaken assumption that if their child acts confused, she has a serious problem. In truth, she could be perfectly normal—just a little immature.

More significantly, Jennifer's glazed looks may give you the clue that whatever readiness means for her, it encompasses her inability to deal with new situations. As long as you have ruled out any physiological or developmental problems, your role is to be supportive until she "gets it." By that we mean that you can do whatever you need to do to enrich Jennifer's environment without putting pressure on her. Give her new experiences. Take her on school visits repeatedly if you have to. Help her but don't ridicule her. Her bewilderment is not her fault.

In Chapter 8, we suggest ways in which you can help your child prepare for and adjust to life in elementary school by offering her opportunities to visit the classroom to get used to normal changes in routine.

Ability to Take Care of Bodily Needs

Ask yourself the following questions:

★ Can my preschooler dress himself?
★ Does he feed himself using the appropriate utensils?
★ Does he use the toilet without having to be reminded or helped?
★ Does he know how to avoid danger?
★ Can he distinguish among feeling hungry, sleepy, and sick?
★ Does he know to ask for help if he's not feeling well?
★ Can he indicate which body part is hurting?
★ Does he take care of his belongings?

Some of these may sound absurd, yet all of these skills indicate some measure of physical independence on your preschooler's part. While each of these is important, however, you may want to ask yourself a larger question: *Is my preschooler willing and able to take care of himself?*

Again, you are faced with a question of maturity here. We remember instances, for example, when our younger daughter, Aimee, would reverse her shoes (the left shoe on the right foot and vice versa) and walk around the house wondering why the heck she was so uncomfortable. No amount of cajoling on our part would get her to do it right the next time. Naturally, she grew out of it. Today, as a teenager, she enjoys shopping for and wearing (on the proper foot, we might add) some of the more outlandish shoe styles. Sooner or later, your preschooler will learn to be physically independent. Just remember that this is a maturational issue and quite normal.

Ability to Form an Appropriate Relationship with the Teacher

When our older daughter, Cherie, was nearing the end of her preschool experience, the nursery school director commented on how our five-year-old spent lots of time following her around and talking up a storm. Cherie was extremely verbal (we later discovered that she was highly gifted) and had spent most of her earlier years in purely adult company. The director expressed some concern about our daughter's attachment to adults rather than to her peers. In some ways, it was easier for Cherie to relate to grown-ups than to other kids her age, who didn't quite know what to make of her.

The director felt that Cherie's relationship with her was inappropriate. She was concerned that our daughter would have problems socially as she continued in school. Fortunately, Cherie was able to find a kindred spirit in kindergarten—another little girl with the same abilities and somewhat mature view of the world. The intense friendship these children formed served them both well for several years.

But the nursery school director's point was well taken. Your child's affiliation with her nursery school teacher is in some ways indicative of her future relationships with other adults and other teachers—the kindergarten teacher in particular. After all, the preschool teacher is the first important alliance your child develops outside of parents or parent substitutes, and the kindergarten teacher is, most likely, the second.

What constitutes an appropriate relationship? Mostly it's based on your preschooler's ability to differentiate between teacher and parent and between home and school. Does she understand that the rules and routines at home are different from the ones at school? Is she able to talk to her teacher about her homelife and talk with her parents about her school life? During "Show and Tell," does she bring interesting toys and appropriate objects or her favorite teddy bear that no one else can touch? Appropriate sharing at this time indicates how well she has made the transition from home to school.

If, on the other hand, she feels so close to her teacher that she demands constant physical affection and special, undivided attention, the child may not have differentiated teacher from Mommy in her mind. This may cause her some difficulty in separating from the preschool teacher and from you once it's time for kindergarten. It may cause her to struggle in forming peer relationships.

Again, appropriate relationships with teachers are a question of maturation. In this case, it would be advisable for you to keep in touch with the preschool teacher. She most assuredly should be working with your child, expressing her affection but also pointing out desirable ways for the child to interact with her and with others. Eventually your child will "get it."

Ability to Form Relationships with Classmates

By the time your child enters kindergarten, he should have a good understanding of what it means to share toys and fantasies. Does he know how to take turns and cooperate? Can he compromise and be the daddy instead of insisting on playing the robber when participating in the doll corner? By now, he may also show the beginnings of having a real friend. He may care about another little boy's feelings and want to please him.

Your preschooler will also be aware of the differences among his peers and be able to cope with those dissimilarities. Socioeconomic, cultural, or racial factors may come into play. Can your child adjust to the fact that some kids dress differently than he does or eat unfamiliar foods? Does he understand that being different is not equated with being bad?

Preschool classmates may also have emotional problems—some may be withdrawn while others are quite aggressive. Some may have a physical disability that renders them different (like the need to wear glasses) or frightening (a deformity or injury). Does your preschooler try to understand these differences? Can he cope with and adapt to them? If another child is aggressive, does your child know how to act in a way that protects him from perceived danger? All of these issues are important in your child's capacity to make good judgments about others. This contributes to his ability to form relationships with all kinds of people in his world.

In Chapter 4 we discuss the importance of socialization in your child's readiness for kindergarten. Skilled preschool teachers who have been steeped in child development are well equipped to handle relationship issues among children.

If you find that this area has become a problem, enlist the teacher's guidance. If she is not doing so already, ask her to work with your child to help him understand the concept of cooperation or to help him express his feelings appropriately. The preschool teacher may not have finished the job by the time your child enters elementary school (because each child matures at a different rate), but the kindergarten teacher will most likely pick up the trail where the former teacher has left off.

Ability to Play

Some forms of play create transitions to schoolwork. For example, sitting in a corner and sucking one's finger while rocking in a chair is more "primitive" than playing with toys, painting, or using the jungle gym, all of which incorporate fine and gross motor coordination and socialization skills. Smearing Play-Doh all over the table and making a goopy mess is less oriented toward growth than is sculpting figures out of the stuff.

According to Ms. Furman, more mature play "is in the service of role taking or skill acquisition, in contrast to earlier play which brings instinctual pleasures (compare the child who is earnestly absorbed in producing a picture at the easel with the one who excitedly uses the paints and brush to make a mess)." The end result may not differ appreciably (neither of the children may have produced anything recognizable), but the more immature child will go about his project with an "excited face and jerky wild motions." The astute parent or teacher recognizes these signs and gently guides the preschooler toward clean-up or a calmer activity. Remember that immaturity is neither bad nor good. It just gives a clue as to where the child may need work.

As preschoolers mature, they begin to take pride in the creation of a project. You may want to watch for your child's interest in this area. Does she take pleasure in the actual doing of a project? Does she show pride in its accomplishment? If she experiences these emotions, she may feel motivated to try the project again as she works toward mastery. At each repetition, she hones her skills and becomes more "ready."

Ability to Exert Internal Controls

In order to be a functioning member of society, your preschooler will have to learn to control some of his impulses. In truth, none of us can have everything we want at the moment we want it. We learn to delay gratification, even if it means not eating the moment we feel hunger or not using the bathroom the moment we sense the urge. As your child nears the maturity level that's expected for kindergarten readiness, he should know how to coordinate his needs and appetites with reality and with the expectations of our society.

In a school setting, internal control means learning to share rather than keeping the toys all to himself, or accepting a substitute toy for the one originally chosen; working at a difficult art project without trashing the work in frustration; postponing an activity because it's nap time. His preschool teacher (and perhaps eventually his kindergarten teacher) should be working with him in attaining these goals.

Ability to Recognize, Verbalize, and Tolerate Feelings

Can your preschooler express her own feelings and can she listen to and understand the emotions of those around her? Your child's ability to recognize when she's angry or jealous will help her gain control over her actions. Rather than striking out at the person who engendered these emotions, she can say, "I don't like it when you take away the Big Wheels. It's my turn. You make me *mad*." Recognizing and verbalizing her feelings also provides her with the option of seeking a solution to her problem. To her first statement, she can add, "Can we take turns?"

Your child will encounter other children who haven't learned to use language to express their emotions. They may be more used to acting out their feelings by hitting or pushing. Does your preschooler know how to deal with someone who is hurting her? It should be of some consolation to you to know that your child will continue to work on her social skills in kindergarten and, indeed, throughout her life. They are the basis of her positive relationships with others.

THE BIRTHDATE EFFECT

As if kindergarten readiness wasn't confusing enough, there's also the age factor to consider. Depending on the state in which you live, the cutoff date for kindergarten qualification can be April 1 before the fall term starts or October 31, December 1, January 1, or some other date after the fall term starts. Children who are not yet five by these dates cannot begin the school year. According to the National Association for the Education of Young Children, these arbitrary dates have been chosen for administrative convenience and "to be as fair and as objective as possible in regulating which children are legally old enough to attend kindergarten."

A study team headed by Dr. P. Langer estimated that school systems using the kindergarten entrance age cutoff of five years old by December, January, or February should expect 50 percent of the boys and 25 percent of the girls to be developmentally "not ready." States adhering to fall cutoff dates can expect about a third of the boys to be not ready. California, the state in which we live, falls under the December cutoff. In our family, these dates seemed to have made a significant difference in our daughters' school experiences.

Cherie, our older daughter, was born in February so she was five and a half when she started kindergarten and was among the oldest children in her grade. As we explained earlier, Cherie was a verbal and adult-oriented preschooler—at eighteen months she could recite the alphabet. She was reading by the age of four. Since she was so "advanced" for her age, we thought it might be wise for her to skip elementary kindergarten altogether—we would just start her in the first grade. At four and a half, we put her in her preschool's "kindergarten" group with that goal in mind.

Fortunately, after we moved into our first house when Cherie was five, we discovered several other children in the neighborhood with birthdays in December and January. They were equally bright and became her friends. After much thought and discussion, we decided to keep Cherie with her peers. Only later did we appreciate what a wise decision that was. For Cherie was quite precocious intellectually, but physically and emotionally she was a late bloomer. In the sixth grade, for example, when her classmates were interested in more adolescent pursuits, puberty was still a distant shadow on the horizon for her. Imagine how much harder junior high and high school would have been for her socially had we pushed her ahead when she was five.

Aimee, on the other hand, was born in October. She started kindergarten before her fifth birthday and was one of the "babies" in her class. It seemed that Aimee could never quite get it all together. Sometimes she reminded us of the character Pigpen in the Peanuts comic strip. She was disorganized. She often misconstrued instructions. She lost her papers and her toys—and eventually her books.

As she grew older, Aimee's lack of maturity seemed to plague her feelings of self-worth. She couldn't understand how her friends, who were no brighter than she, could conceptualize material that seemed foreign to her. Her third-grade teacher, impatient with Aimee's having lost her third math book in as many weeks, ridiculed her in front of the class, calling her "stupid." This, as you can imagine, was devastating to our daughter and enraged us, but the damage was done. Mitch, who was also a late-blooming four-year-old when he started kindergarten, understood perfectly. He kept reassuring Aimee that she would catch on eventually.

In more recent years as Aimee passed from the ninth grade into high school, unreadiness still plagued her. Developmentally, she was not ready for algebra or beginning Spanish in the ninth grade, even though they were included in the curriculum recommended for her age. She just couldn't master what was being taught. To her, none of it made any sense. After only two weeks, she was failing the algebra class. That was no way to begin her experience with math, so we saw to it that Aimee was transferred into pre-algebra. She finished out the year of Spanish with a D.

The following year, full of trepidation, Aimee tried algebra and Spanish once more. This time she got As and Bs. The subjects certainly hadn't gotten any easier in the interim. But Aimee was able to conceptualize the material now. Her difficulties had had little to do with her intelligence. There is no question that she is bright enough; it had been a developmental issue all along. She just wasn't ready earlier.

The point we're making here is that age and maturation are very tricky issues. None of us can predict how our children will develop. What seems like a good idea now may prove to be a mistake later, and vice versa. Would Aimee have been better off if we had delayed the start of kindergarten for a year? Perhaps. But we have no way of knowing how that would have affected her socially. Her best friend, Alix, began elementary school on the same day Aimee did. Alix's birthday was only one month before Aimee's. Would it not have been more devastating to our daughter to feel left behind by her peers?

These are questions each of us has to answer for ourselves in the context of our own families. Short of planning the births of your children around the kindergarten entrance cutoff date, the issues are quite complex and don't yield to simple solutions.

According to the National Association for the Education of Young Children's report on kindergarten readiness, research has established that "younger children in the group do have a slightly more difficult time academically in kindergarten and throughout the elementary years." The report cites many studies as substantiation. Children—especially boys—entering kindergarten at the younger end of the spectrum

★ have more academic problems.
★ have more learning difficulties.
★ have lower standardization test scores.
★ are more likely to fail a grade.

Some studies trace the results of this "birthdate effect" through junior high school and even adult life.

It would seem, then, that delaying school entrance a year so that these children have time to mature would solve the problem. Jane Zuckerman, a nursery school director for a large preschool in Los Angeles, feels that it may be beneficial to retain socially immature four-year-olds and five-year-olds in preschool in the hope that the extra year of maturity will resolve these issues. She suggests that changing to a new nursery school for that additional year can take away some of the stigma of being retained.

Other experts, such as child psychoanalyst Erna Furman, believe that children don't progress or lag behind uniformly. They may function appropriately in some areas and inappropriately in others. "It is a common mistake to attribute these lags and deviations to 'immaturity' and to assume that time—especially in the form of an extra year in nursery school—will enable the child to 'catch up.' " Without a careful treatment program established among teacher, parents, and child to deal with the reason for the delay, an extra year can serve to "lock in" the problems so that they become more severe and less accessible to amelioration.

What about the child deemed "not ready" who does not attend an appropriate preschool? According to Dr. Rosalind Charlesworth of Louisiana State University, "The problem with delaying school entry for those 'not ready' is obvious: By excluding them from rich learning experiences, they become progressively 'behinder and behinder.' " The National Association for the Education of Young Children concurs and adds its own arguments against delayed entry. As they put it:

> The problem for some of these children often does not surface for several years: They are older and more mature than their classmates and become bored. This not infrequently leads to lowered motivation to do what the class is doing and to behavior problems. In making decisions about kindergarten, the long term must be considered, too.

Another alternative is to place young kindergarteners in transition or pre-kindergarten classes, which have been springing up around the country lately. This approach, unfortunately, is not entirely acceptable either. According to the National Association for the Education of Young Children, "Children in these transition or pre-K classes are often labeled as 'slow,' an image that may stick with them throughout their school lives. Teachers, parents, other children, and even the children themselves may have lower expectations for success."

Besides, the pre-K class may not make much of a difference. According to the same report, "Children from transitional programs do about as well in first grade as other children enrolled in kindergarten at a young age."

Having a child repeat kindergarten seems no better a solution, for the child runs the risk of being labeled a failure. Again, teachers, parents, and the child himself will lower their expectations.

WHAT IF YOUR CHILD ISN'T "READY"?

One of the most difficult aspects of parenting is the feeling of powerlessness that we get from time to time. We want our children to feel successful. We want them to enjoy what they're doing and to feel good about themselves. Maybe we have a secret wish that their positive experience will make up for whatever we regret in our own lives—that they will be able to go to Harvard even though we couldn't, for example. These feelings are natural. But when our children's development and maturation don't match our hopes and expectations, we are disappointed and we experience our own limitedness.

In making any decision affecting your preschooler's placement, it is important to proceed slowly and carefully. If you and the preschool director and teacher agree that your child is ready for kindergarten, there is no problem. If, on the other hand, there is some question, it might be helpful to use a test to help clarify in which areas your child is strong and in which she is weaker. (We have much more on testing in the next chapter.) But the test itself should not be used as a yardstick.

As nursery school director Jane Zuckerman emphasizes, "When the child isn't ready, it's not a surprise. We should see it all the way along the line and the parents should be informed."

If your child has not been enrolled in a preschool, however, and has scored "not ready" at a kindergarten screening, make sure that you communicate with the staff at the elementary school. According to the National Association for the Education of Young Children report, "Sometimes the [pre-K] groups are established without close consultation with parents, who have a wealth of information about their children that might indicate a more appropriate and different placement." Explore all of the available options, including placement in a pre-K class or even a private kindergarten, and take into consideration any long-term consequences that can come from your decision.

Finally, your best solution may be to approach your local school board and state board of education with complaints about how the system has been set up in the first place. If enough parents complain, perhaps these public institutions will reexamine their policies. Again, to quote from the National Association for the Education of Young Children report:

> In any or all of these patchwork, quick-fix approaches to the problem, the most important factor is overlooked: the curriculum itself. Children are being blamed for their inability to keep pace with the curriculum. Instead of looking at entry criteria, we should be reexamining the curriculum to see whether it is appropriate for the children, because all children succeed when the curriculum is appropriate.

CHAPTER 3

To Test or Not to Test . . .

Can we justify testing preschoolers? Yes, there is a place for screening tests—especially those that measure the child's physiological functioning. Within very strict limits we can also justify the use of developmental and other "readiness" tests. But we feel, as we will explain below, that the latter should not be the exclusive criterion for measuring whether your preschooler is ready for school. More on that in a moment. First, let's look at the kinds of tests we do feel are always helpful.

THE IMPORTANCE OF EARLY PHYSIOLOGICAL TESTING

Mitch was born with extraordinary myopia. His right eye is not correctable with glasses. He was deferred from military service during the Vietnam era because of his poor vision. The government was afraid that if he lost his glasses, he would not know who the enemy was. (Indeed, his vision without glasses is so poor, he probably wouldn't have been able to find the jungle!)

Mitch's visual problems were discovered when he was about three years old. His parents noticed that he kept bumping into doors and falling off furniture. For Mitch, not being able to see was a frightening experience. He felt inadequate because he could not pick up the information around him. His world was limited. Today, he has no way of knowing how his self-confidence could have been enhanced had the problem been diagnosed earlier.

Children who experience physiological problems like vision or hearing loss often struggle to make connections with the world around them. Ironically, until their condition is detected, they have no way to recognize that a deficiency exists. This stands to reason. A preschooler who can't see well doesn't know what seeing well means. He thinks that everyone experiences the world in the same way he does.

Unfortunately, such physiological problems can impede socialization and eventual academic achievement. According to Dr. Anne Panofsky, a Los Angeles clinical psychologist who is herself hearing-impaired:

> Children who have a hearing loss may feel anxious, rigid, or excluded from the world of their peers. They don't experience the environment in the same way as their friends since they don't receive input on all "channels." It's difficult for them to integrate all that is going on around them. As a result, they may withdraw or they may become controlling.

Such children can lose out on all-important social interactions. Their self-esteem then suffers. And as we all know, positive self-esteem benefits a child's intelligence and achievement.

In addition, if your child can't hear the teacher or see the blackboard, she will have a hard time keeping up with the rest of the class. Indeed, according to Dr. Panofsky, some studies have revealed that hearing-impaired children were once mistakenly classified as mentally retarded since they had withdrawn and couldn't participate in regular classroom activities.

It becomes clear, then, that you should have your preschooler's vision and hearing tested before she enters kindergarten. Nursery school directors recommend a visual screening by an ophthalmologist—not just the simple eye chart at the pediatrician's or school nurse's office. Hearing should be tested by an audiologist in a soundproof booth.

Sometimes preschoolers' social problems are rooted in other physiological disabilities. An asthmatic child, for example, may be teased and ridiculed because he can't keep up physically. A hyperactive child becomes disruptive and earns the ire of his teacher and fellow classmates alike. A child who experiences dyslexia (the perceived reversal of letters and words) may feel stupid and frustrated because he can't tell the difference between a b and a d. He may act out his poor self-concept and frustration with anger.

While some of these problems can't be cured, their early detection will ensure that at least they are properly addressed during your child's school career. Your focus should be on helping your pre-schooler adapt in the face of his apparent problem.

Perhaps you feel something may be amiss with your child but you're not sure what it is. You know your children best. You have feelings and intuitions about them. After all, the doctor and nursery school director don't live in your home with you. If you suspect that something is wrong, don't be put off by reassurances to the contrary. Seek a second and third opinion—an eighth opinion, if necessary. If there is a children's hospital in your city or community, avail yourself of the services of the specialists there. The earlier disabilities are diagnosed, the sooner corrective action can be taken and, thus, the better for your child.

While we're on the topic of disabilities, we must mention denial. It is exceedingly painful to realize that your child has a problem. Most parents experience such a discovery as a devastating wound to their own egos. Unconsciously they fear that if their children are imperfect then they must be imperfect, too, or that the problem stems directly from something they have done. All of us want to believe that our kids are OK. Sometimes, because of our need to deny that a problem exists, we may not present the full picture to our pediatrician.

In order to help sidestep this natural tendency and to test out your hunch that your child is not developing at the proper pace, you might keep a log of your observations. Usually the symptoms parents describe to health professionals are of such a general nature that the doctor can't make a diagnosis; for example, "It always seems like Jimmy has ants in his pants." There's a fine line, for instance, separating a hyperactive child from a normal but rambunctious five-year-old. Your more precise anecdotal record—such as reporting that within a 60-minute period, Jimmy kept still for only 15 minutes—can make a difference.

Don't fall into the trap of being a Monday morning quarterback. You can avoid the tragic plaint, "If only we had done something sooner . . ." Trust yourself on this. If you sense that something is wrong, do what you can to get it diagnosed and treated.

THE "HIGH-STAKES" TESTS: DEVELOPMENTAL AND READINESS SCREENINGS

A recent "My Turn" editorial in *Newsweek* drew our attention because it brings into focus the dilemma facing many parents of preschoolers today. In it, author Paul Wilkes explains how he had escaped to the New England countryside from the big city—in part to avoid the "intense burden of competition that too many parents seem to load on their kids these days."

One day his six-year-old Noah was summoned to the local elementary school for a "screening."

> He got an 86. A solid B. The school had explained it was a test to see if he was ready for kindergarten; it would also determine if he needed help in any special area. That sounded like a good idea, but when I saw a grade, it was a whole new ball game. This was measurement, standing, placement. Judgment.

This father's response is absolutely normal. It is difficult to look upon any screening of your child as anything less than a measure of who he is as a person. To view tests this way, however, is folly. No school readiness tests are very reliable (that is, the results may vary widely from one testing session to the next), nor are they particularly valid (they don't necessarily test what they purport to test).

According to the National Association for the Education of Young Children's report on kindergarten readiness, "It is alarming to note that school readiness tests *all* have error rates in the range of 50%; that is, half of the children placed in special programs based on results of readiness tests should be enrolled in regular programs." It would be just as accurate (and probably much cheaper) to simply flip a coin.

The association goes on to point out that "findings of many studies clearly lead to the conclusion that although readiness tests may describe what children are like *on the day they take the test*, they cannot predict how children will do in any program. . . . Despite these well-documented shortcomings, readiness tests are commonly used to predict whether children will succeed in kindergarten."

False readings can and do occur. "Some children who have problems are not identified, while other children are referred for further diagnosis because they appear to have problems when they really don't." Most commonly, parents of a child scoring "not ready" are told to delay kindergarten entrance for a year, or the child is placed in a transition or pre-K class, as we discussed in the previous chapter.

In a front-page *New York Times* article on the testing controversy, Dr. Samuel J. Meisels, professor of education at the Center for Human Growth and Development in Ann Arbor, Michigan, calls the misuse of these tests "shockingly high." He estimates that 20 percent of all first-graders are at least a year overage for their grade.

In general, developmental and readiness tests for preschoolers cover the areas of:

★ Fine and gross motor coordination
★ Perceptual skills (like eye-hand coordination)
★ Immediate recall
★ Language development
★ Personal-social behaviors
★ Ability to recognize and process sequences
★ Ability to listen and follow directions
★ Recognition of how objects are the same or different
★ Identification of body parts and their function
★ Naming of common objects and their function

Developmental tests were once viewed as the first step in determining which children had possible handicaps or disabilities. Those preschoolers whose tests showed the potential of problems underwent further diagnostic examination. Readiness screenings were originally constructed as diagnostic tools to help teachers plan the curriculum. For example, if tests showed that seven children in the incoming class didn't know all the colors, the kindergarten teacher knew she should teach about gray, pink, and purple.

Today, unfortunately, these same screenings have come to be used inappropriately as pass-fail standards for kindergarten entrance. This, as we will see, is hurting many children.

Like other changes in our educational system, the misuse of tests has developed over the decades. During the '60s and '70s there was a surge of interest in testing preschoolers before they entered kindergarten. The Head Start program, created to help make up for socioeconomic and cultural deprivation, was one of the factors that contributed to the increase in testing.

Children enrolled in Head Start are unable to attend preschool. They come from homes in which there is not enough money for food, let alone books, crayons, toy trucks, dolls, or blocks. The federal government originally mandated screening tests to help identify children at risk for gross learning disabilities and health problems so that they could receive specialized attention early on.

In the 1980s, with the increase in academic expectations for kindergarteners that we discussed in Chapter 1, more and more children began experiencing kindergarten failure and retention. The concomitant push for teacher accountability, and the greater use of standardized tests in general, seemed to make screening for kindergarten readiness the next logical step.

In effect, once more we encounter the problem we discussed in the previous chapter: Rather than readjust the curriculum to make it more carefully match young children's abilities, school districts have decided to use tests, which were never meant to designate school placement, to determine exactly that—whether or not a child should begin kindergarten.

Screening has become a popular but misguided attempt to help children avoid the possibility of kindergarten "failure" and the need to repeat the year. It has the added "benefit" of weeding out children who can't handle first-grade curriculum at age five—so that academic expectations for kindergarteners are inappropriately inflated yet again. This is a frustrating situation. No wonder the developmentalists are screaming bloody murder!

In order to more fully understand why these tests should not be used to determine placement, let's examine in more detail the two types of tests that school districts generally use today: developmental and readiness screenings.

GESELL DEVELOPMENTAL SCREENINGS

The most frequently used developmental tests are those based on the work of Arnold Gesell and administered by the Gesell Institute. About 20 years ago, Dr. Gesell and his colleagues observed groups of 50 boys and 50 girls per age level and determined that certain behaviors are "normal" at particular ages. The children were mostly Caucasian and lived in Connecticut.

Today, 18 percent of all school districts in the nation use the Gesell School Readiness Tests. During these screening tests your child may be asked to:

★ Arrange ten one-inch cubes into designated structures

★ Answer questions about his age, birthdate, members of the family, your job, and other family matters

★ Using pencil and paper, copy different geometric shapes and forms

★ Write his name

★ Write numbers in order from 1 to 20

★ Complete a rather primitive drawing of a man

★ Name all the animals he can think of in 60 seconds

★ Talk about what he likes to do at home, at school, indoors and outdoors

In evaluating the test, the examiner will look at how the tasks were completed:

★ With which hand(s) and in which direction does he build the block structures? Is a demonstration necessary?

★ How well versed and how spontaneous is your child during the family interview? Can he identify the month and date of his birthday?

★ Can he remember and respond to questions that have one or two parts?

★ How does he hold the paper and grip the pencil, and where does he place the shapes on the paper?

★ How closely does he reproduce the shapes?

★ How accurately does he write numbers? Does he reverse them or write them out of order?

★ Where does he begin the copying and writing exercises: top or bottom? In what direction does he write the numbers: right to left or left to right?

★ How accurately and completely does he complete the drawing of the man? Does he work too much on one area and ignore others? Are eyes and limbs drawn in symmetrically? Does he elaborate on parts of the body or add clothes?

★ Can he name animals for the full 60 seconds? Does he include unusual zoo animals? Does he divide the animals into categories such as fish or fowl?

★ Is he specific about favorite activities at home or school?

The score is given in terms of a "developmental age," or DA. A five-year-old, for example, could have a developmental age of "young five," "five," or "five with evidence of five-and-a-half" behavior.

Problems with the Gesell Screenings

Why do developmentalists say that this test is not a valid way of determining whether a child is ready for kindergarten? To an untrained eye, it certainly seems as if it should be. Well, there are lots of reasons.

To begin with, the test is subjective—there are no wrong or right answers to choose from. That means that your child's score is purely dependent on the examiner's interpretation, experience, training, and judgment. If the examiner has had a bad morning with his own family, if he's new on the job, if he's not quite astute enough to pick up all of your child's cues, his perspective may be somewhat clouded. The same test given by different examiners will yield different scores, depending on how each examiner interprets your child's behavior.

The tests are difficult to administer—and this is true for any screening—because preschoolers have the attention span of a flash-bulb, are apt to get tired, and generally are not interested in taking tests. They may be frightened by new surroundings or the fact that an unfamiliar adult is giving them orders. They may have no idea what is expected of them.

A distraught family who came into Mitch's practice for a consultation about their daughter, Marjorie, illustrates just this point. This bright little girl had "failed" the developmental screening, and her parents were beside themselves with grief and anxiety. Mitch decided to ask Marjorie why she didn't perform on the test.

"That lady asked the dumbest questions!" the five-year-old exclaimed. "Of course I knew my birthday and address. I didn't like the way she talked to me. She hardly smiled at me and she wasn't friendly at all."

Having learned the truth, Marjorie's parents petitioned the school for a retesting with someone else. The preschooler now "passed" with flying colors.

Your child's scores may also be affected by shifts in environment like divorce, illness, a new sibling, or other changes in family structure. Even a sleepless night or a thunderstorm can have a negative effect.

Even normal children who don't experience traumatic events develop in fits and starts and at very different rates. A child who is tested in the spring before entering kindergarten may show up as being immature. Yet, so much growth can occur over the summer that by the time he is ready for school in the fall, he has caught up with his classmates. If the test has determined that he is developmentally delayed, however, he may be inappropriately retained in preschool for another year.

Critics of the Gesell tests point out that results are often used to label children even if the scores are not valid. According to one vociferous opponent, Dr. Samuel Meisels of Ann Arbor, Michigan,

the Gesell tests "are based on an outmoded theory of child development, lack reliability and validity, and use a concept of developmental
age that has never been empirically verified." Other critics mention
the fact that the original groups of children observed were inadequate for Dr. Gesell to draw such broad conclusions about what is
"normal." At the very least, the groups displayed little ethnic or
sociocultural diversity.

There are also more technical objections to the test's scoring
system. Dr. Sue Bredekamp, director of professional development at
the National Association for the Education of Young Children, and
Dr. Lorrie Shepard, professor of education at the University of Col-
orado, complain that there are no standards against which to judge
the scores. "It is not possible to tell whether a child's performance is
normal. A 5-year-old child who performs like an average 4½-year-old
is treated as if he were seriously deficient, yet for all the tester
knows, that child's score is at the 40th or 45th percentile of all five-
year-olds, and therefore quite normal." (The 45th percentile means
that 45 percent of the children who took the test scored lower.)

In addition, developmentalists argue that a child's scores on the
Gesell tests cannot and do not predict how that child will fare in
kindergarten. Again, Drs. Bredekamp and Shepard make the point
most strongly:

> Using even the most favorable data, the Gesell test misidentified ⅓
> to ½ of children said to be unready. . . . Correlations of this same
> size would be obtained if *parents* were given an IQ test and the
> result correlated with each *child's* first grade scores. Would it then
> be valid to place children on the basis of the parents' measured IQ?
> Of course not.

How Can Educators Use the Gesell Tests More Effectively?

According the Anna Anastasi, a leading expert in the field of
psychological testing and author of a testing "bible" entitled *Psychological Testing,* now in its sixth printing, the Gesell schedules "appear to be most useful as a supplement to medical examinations for
the identification of neurological defect and organically caused behavior abnormalities in early life." The tests are not as useful as a
measure of variations among normal preschoolers. Results should be
coupled with a pediatrician's observations, parents' input, and the
nursery school staff's evaluation in order to be most effective.

Others stress that the Gesell tests should be used as they were originally intended: to help teachers assess children's abilities and needs so that they can plan classroom activities appropriately. According to Drs. Bredekamp and Shepard, "When a test is used to plan instruction within a classroom, it does not have to be as accurate as a test that is used for placement."

READINESS SCREENINGS

Kindergarten readiness screening tests are somewhat different from the developmental tests discussed above. These screenings purport to measure a child's achievement in academic areas—that is, how well she knows specific academic subject matter. Think of them as the first in a long line of achievement tests that culminate in the twelfth grade with the Scholastic Aptitude Test (SAT) and the Achievement exams given in specific subject areas like biology or French. They don't measure intelligence—just how much a child "knows."

The most commonly used screening device for kindergarten is the Metropolitan Readiness Tests (MRT). In these tests, your preschooler will be working from a test booklet. She will be asked to:

★ Identify specific letters of the alphabet
★ Match identical visual images (as in "one of these things is just like the others" from "Sesame Street")
★ Follow directions given as verbal commands and match what has been said with material in the booklet
★ Do simple math word problems
★ Identify rhyming words (by choosing pictures of items that "sound alike")

She may be required to demonstrate prereading skills. In those tests, she would be asked to:

★ Understand and identify beginning consonant sounds
★ Match a sound to its corresponding letter
★ Identify visual patterns
★ Show that she understands the correlation between numbers and numerals (i.e., that the numeral 5 represents five dogs)
★ Do simple addition and subtraction problems

Problems with Readiness Screening Tests

Again, developmentalists question whether these tests should be used to keep children out of kindergarten. According to Sue Bredekamp and Lorrie Shepard, the Metropolitan Readiness Tests are between 70 percent and 78 percent valid in predicting how a child will do in the first grade.

Although these correlations are impressively high if the test is used for instructional planning or program evaluation as intended by its authors, they nonetheless indicate that as many as one-third of children would be misidentified as "unready" if the MRT were used for kindergarten placement.

THE FALLOUT FROM TESTING

Unfortunately, all of this information about the inappropriateness of developmental and readiness screenings is not being heeded in many preschools and school districts. According to the *New York Times* article we mentioned earlier, "These tests are increasingly being misused as admissions tests and children who do not do well are being forced to put off starting school."

Lydia Richards, supervisor of quality assurance in the division of monitoring and evaluation of the New York State Department of Education, explains that "research shows that children who are behind even one year have a significant increase in being at risk of not completing high school." Other experts indicate that by the third grade, maturational differences even out anyway, and retaining a child does more psychological harm than good. Socially, your youngster's self-esteem will suffer if he does not join his peers in kindergarten or if he is the oldest among his classmates later.

Those risks are further increased by a preschooler's being pigeonholed as "immature" or "slow." If your child has been labeled as less adequate than his peers, he may begin to believe it, even if he is only a late bloomer. Such self-fulfilling prophecies can be damaging. If you say he is "slow," then he will act in accordance with that label. You require less of him, his self-esteem is lowered, and he repeats his poor performance because that's what is expected of him.

Indeed, child psychoanalyst Erna Furman makes the point that children experience a maturational drive to learn and to work.

If the child's educational environment does not provide adequate support and scope for this drive, it subsides and cannot be recaptured later. A child who starts academic learning and working when he is a year or two older does not necessarily catch on faster. He may actually learn more slowly and with less zest because he has missed out on utilizing the crest of maturational learning drive and on developing basic learning skills.

SHOULD YOU COACH YOUR CHILD?

Admittedly, you are in a difficult situation here and the answers can't come easily. Should you try to prepare your child for developmental or screening tests by coaching him in the material that will be tested? Books such as *The Baby Boards: A Parents' Guide to Preschool and Primary School Entrance Exams* by Jacqueline Robinson purport to "teach your 3- to 5-year-old skills needed to win admission to selective early schooling programs." Yet, they have been roundly criticized by developmentalists as being inappropriate.

Assuming that your preschooler can be "taught" to take a developmental test, for example, so what if he now starts writing his numbers from the left instead of the right? Such discrete bits of information or skills make little sense when they are not integrated with the rest of the child.

In addition, your coaching would, for all intents and purposes, invalidate the test. The scoring for such tests is based on all children being in the same boat. The test is constructed with the expectation that the test-takers have never seen it before. Any score that your child would receive as a result of your coaching would not truly reflect his abilities or his developmental maturity. That could be detrimental to him in the long run, because his teachers' expectations may be based on the invalid perception that he actually understands the developmental concepts reflected in the questions.

WHAT'S TO BE DONE?

Ideally, elementary schools should base their decisions about kindergarten placement not on a single test (if tests are going to be used) but rather on a broad range of factors, including:

★ The child's birthdate
★ The results of screening or diagnostic tests for curriculum purposes
★ Parents' input

★ The pediatrician's observations
★ The preschool teacher's recommendations

Your perspective may be the most important part of the equation. You know Katie best. You can share with the school administrators any situations at home or health issues that could affect her performance on a test—or in school, for that matter. You can discuss her personality and help the administrators to judge the test scores within the larger context of your child's overall development. *For your child's own good, you must make it your business to get involved!*

You can get involved in a larger way by lobbying for change within your community. Drs. Bredekamp and Shepard reported on a 1988 case in the Norwood-Norfolk school district in New York. That district had assigned a whopping 61 percent of all incoming kindergarteners to a two-year developmental kindergarten on the basis of a single administration of the Gesell.

The parents in this district organized themselves and sued the schools, claiming that the developmental set-up was essentially a "special placement" and that the children's rights had been denied. (Federal and state statutes mandate that special placements can be made only with individualized educational evaluations, multiple testing, due process, and the informed consent of the parents.) You'll be happy to know that the parents won. The New York State Department of Education put the children back into a regular kindergarten and the school district has since revised its placement policies.

If you are to rally for a change in screening and placement policies, the National Association for the Education of Young Children recommends that you ask your school district to:

★ Select only tests that are valid and reliable.
★ Use those tests only for their intended purposes and in conjunction with other assessment.
★ Involve parents in the evaluation process.
★ Consider the readiness results as only *one* source of information to help in curriculum planning.
★ Never use the tests to determine placement.
★ Gather information about the children's progress regularly and from many sources.

Finally, in the words of the National Association for the Education of Young Children:

> Tests cannot tell us: what thinking processes children use to solve problems; whether children's curiosity is being enhanced; what strategies children use to get along with each other; whether children can appreciate beauty and diversity in the world around them; how kind children are to others; whether children are persistent in real situations; or whether children have a growing sense of responsibility for themselves and others. Tests do not, and cannot, measure the broad scope of what children are learning.

CHAPTER 4

The First R of Kindergarten Readiness: Developing Relationships

As you can see, your preschooler's performance on so-called readiness screenings has only limited value in predicting how he will fare in kindergarten. On the other hand, your child's ability to develop meaningful relationships with others—his socialization skill—is essential for his success in kindergarten and thereafter. *Socialization* is a rather clinical term that you may be hearing a lot of as you prepare your child for school. In a nutshell, socialization means how children get along with others.

Please consider the following indications of socialization as a continuum. We know many an adult who has yet to master all of these aspects of social interaction. Nevertheless, a well-socialized child:

★ Is happy in the company of other children and comfortable around adults

★ Is able to express his feelings and acknowledges the feelings of others

★ Is able to get his needs met by using words appropriately

★ Knows how to share materials, time, and space and respects the property of others

★ Abides by the rules and limits (morals, if you will) of your family and culture and learns right from wrong

★ Is courteous and considerate

★ Feels good about himself
★ Can assert himself but can also accept the leadership of others

PARENTING: THE ORIGIN OF SOCIAL BEHAVIOR

Your child's socialization begins at birth when you pick her up and begin talking and smiling to her, when you sing and make eye contact, when you create a warm and loving bond with her. You are teaching your baby that the world is a friendly place and that she can trust you to be there in an affectionate and gentle way. She feels safe and secure. She smiles and gurgles, encouraging you to talk and play with her all the more. When she sees that she has a positive effect on you, she feels valued. She begins to feel good about herself. Indeed, socialization builds self-esteem, and self-esteem underlies your child's eventual success in school and in all other facets of life.

As we explained in our book *Disciplining Your Preschooler and Feeling Good About It,* socialization also means that your child understands and abides by the rules and limits created by your family and society. For your preschooler, these might include: No pinching, spitting, kicking, biting, or pulling hair. Wait your turn without shoving. Share. Express your feelings in words. Use your fork and spoon and eat with your mouth closed and your elbows off the table. Never run into the street. Don't cross a street without holding an adult's hand. Don't pull Kitty's tail.

These rules are what transform your baby from a mass of quivering protoplasm to a functioning member of our society. In fact, every family in every culture has rules and limits of this sort. Otherwise, life would be chaos for us all. Anthropologists and social psychologists have discerned thirteen areas in which all cultures create standards for proper socialization:

Eating
Excreting
Sexuality
Aggression
Dependence and independence
Emotional development and attachment to others
Achievement
Competition and cooperation
Sense of individuality
Life and death

Mating

Pain

Right and wrong

You teach your preschooler about these rules by setting an example and by creating limits and following through with appropriate consequences. Your guidance is necessary. Otherwise your preschooler will have a hard time keeping friends and getting along with others in her world. Children who are socially competent have the ability to form and maintain positive relationships with other children. Your role as a parent is to set the stage for and reinforce the social learning that occurs at preschool and kindergarten.

WHAT SHOULD YOU LOOK FOR IN YOUR CHILD'S BEHAVIOR?

Child developmentalists and early-childhood educators mark the following milestones in social development for four- to five-year-olds. An appropriately socialized preschooler:

1. Plays cooperatively with others.
2. Enjoys friends, and is willing to share them.
3. Participates in dramatic play, and can take on a variety of roles.
4. Asks many questions (including the ubiquitous "Why?") and is genuinely interested in your responses.
5. "Catches" behavior from other children. (If one five-year-old starts blowing bubbles in her milk, all of her friends will follow suit.)
6. Brags about having the "best" and "biggest."
7. Tests limits by defying your guidelines.
8. Tells tall tales. (Most preschoolers don't lie, they just haven't mastered the difference between fact and fiction.)
9. Uses "dirty" language, sometimes when angry and sometimes for fun.

HOW YOU "TEACH" SOCIALIZATION

What if your child is having trouble with cooperative play or understanding what it means to share? While there are no easy answers and we can't offer you a checklist ticking off specific socialization strategies, it is important to be aware that subtle and overt communications from you do guide your child's social adjustment all the time.

To begin with, we all teach by example and our children learn by mimicking us. Think back on how your child learned how to speak. He listened and then tried to repeat the sounds as best he could. Eventually he got "Mama" and "Dada" right and was rewarded for his efforts with your hugs and kisses and squeals of delight. That motivated him to try again.

As a preschooler, your child still learns by imitation. He listens and watches your social interactions with him and with others in his world. If you are always hostile and angry, he may decide that this is how people act with one another, and he'll do the same. If, on the other hand, he observes your kindness and sharing, eventually (children are still quite self-centered at this age) he will learn to build on the model you have presented.

You also teach socialization skills to your child in your daily interactions with him. An incident from a recent trip to the beach illustrates this point.

We were lounging on our blanket, happy in the thought that we no longer have to keep sand out of our kids' mouths and eyes or be vigilant about their status vis-à-vis the ocean (at 16 and 20 years of age, they no longer deign to accompany us to the beach). We observed a young mother and son on the blanket next to ours. The little boy, Timmy, seemed about three years old. He had spread his sand toys out—the pail and shovel at one end of the blanket and his sand rake at the other.

This latter, seemingly abandoned toy posed the perfect invitation to Camille, a three-year-old ensconced one blanket beyond. Unable to hold herself back, she wandered over, picked up Timmy's rake, and began digging with it.

The little boy was upset. He went straight to his mom. "Mommy," he cried, "she took my rake!"

Timmy's mother, nonplussed, replied, "You had better take it away from her. Go on, get it, Timmy."

Timmy tried but he got elbowed in the ribs for his efforts. "That's mine," he yelled at the little girl, to no avail. Then he turned back to his mom in frustration. "Mommy, she still won't give it!"

His mother replied, "You either take it away from her or I guess you're leaving here without it."

Poor Timmy looked anxious and perplexed. He was about to try to grab the rake out of the little girl's hand one more time when *her* mother intervened. "Camille," she said, "that toy belongs to this boy. You can't take things that aren't yours. Now give it back to him." Camille did.

These mothers, each in her own way, were teaching their children certain social skills. Timmy was learning to be more assertive (survival of the fittest?) while Camille was learning that she could not appropriate someone else's things, no matter how attractive. It was none of our business, but we would have preferred Timmy's mom to spend some time talking about cooperation and sharing ("Let the little girl play with it for five minutes while you're not using it"). Not knowing this family well, however, we were in no place to judge. Nevertheless, it was clear that socialization was going on right before our eyes. Every day in a hundred ways, socialization occurs in your family, as well.

PRESCHOOL IS A GREAT SOCIALIZER

Your child doesn't learn social skills from you alone. She also picks them up from siblings, playmates, other adult family members such as uncles or grandmothers, baby-sitters—in fact, everyone with whom she comes in contact.

Preschool is a rich resource for learning social skills as well. There, your child has many children with whom to interact and she also benefits from the guidance of teachers trained in early-childhood development who ease the way. In fact, because of its impact on social development, we recommend preschool as an important part of getting your child ready for kindergarten. If that is out of the question for your family, we offer other recommendations in the next section of this chapter.

For the moment, let's examine a simple group project to understand why preschool is so enriching. The activity: the stringing of wooden beads of various sizes, shapes, and colors done by a cluster of children sitting at one table. This seemingly innocuous game imparts information about a myriad of subjects and helps to develop social as well as intellectual skills.

★ Children begin to appreciate the differences among objects and organize them according to their sameness or difference, an essential for letter recognition.

★ They count the beads and recognize shapes in preparation for doing arithmetic.

★ They use their fine motor coordination, which will be so important when they begin learning to hold a pencil properly and write.
★ They learn colors and enjoy creating something that they regard as beautiful.

Best of all, as they are engaged in fashioning their masterpieces, they hoard, trade, or share beads; copy each other's patterns and designs; discuss and compare their results. In other words, they are busy practicing socialization skills because they are working and playing with each other.

Lilian Katz, professor of early-childhood education at the University of Illinois, has stated that "young children's learning is enhanced when they are engaged in interactive processes. . . . In addition to learning through trial and error and through observation, young children gain a great deal cognitively as well as socially in the course of interacting with each other, with adults, and with aspects of their environment."

Dr. Katz gives a wonderful example of a complex group project that she heard about indirectly. A class of kindergarteners undertook the study of their own school bus. She surmised that they divided up into groups, some examining the driving mechanisms (the motor, radiator, and other working parts under the hood), others studying the gauges and pedals at the driver's seat, still others inspecting how the bus's door operated, which was surely different from any door in their homes. Then she imagined that the group reunited to explain and discuss their findings and eventually constructed their own "bus" in the classroom. The whole undertaking could have spanned a week or two.

Such a project, while relatively sophisticated for preschoolers, has elements essential for social and intellectual growth. The children involved were interested in and interacting with their own environment over an extended period of time. The hands-on approach meant that they were getting real-life experience rather than a lecture. The children's vocabulary expanded as they learned the names of the various parts of the vehicle. The activity sharpened the kids' observation skills as well. In addition, the bus provided a terrific subject for conversation. This last point is significant.

Many researchers agree that the preschool years are a crucial time for the development of communication and language. Children learn to express themselves and to understand others. They put their feelings into words and use language to get their wants and needs met. Conversations are important in developing intellectual and social abilities as well, since children learn to follow one idea with the next when discussing problems and ideas with their peers. We will cover this important topic more fully in Chapter 6.

Not all preschools are equally successful in teaching socialization skills. If you are concerned about the one your child is currently attending or if you're looking for a new preschool, keep in mind the following questions.

Are Learning Activities Geared Toward Socialization?

There are a million possible activities for preschoolers. The essential issue is whether the intellectual activity has a social basis. Sitting around in a circle and identifying flashcards of letters is not a social activity! Rather, the teacher should use reading-readiness skills as a source of group play. Look for a preschool that stresses the importance of the group as a learning community.

Does the Staff Address Each Child's Personal Needs?

Each child is unique, with his own set of interests and needs. David has a new brother at home and is acting more aggressive at school, while Janie's parents are going through a divorce and she is withdrawing into her shell. Observe (during a school visit or when you drop off or pick up your preschooler) whether the teachers take the time to ascertain what kind of attention each child needs. Does the teacher address your child's problems directly?

Does the Teacher Get Down to the Children's Level?

Adults are large and loud to preschoolers and can seem intimidating. Observe whether the teacher literally gets down to the children's level and makes eye contact as she speaks to them. Is there gentle and appropriate physical contact as well, especially when a child is hurting?

Does the Staff Help Children Put Their Feelings into Words?

Not all preschoolers are adept at expressing themselves clearly. This is a skill learned through practice over time. The teachers should ask children what they mean or how they feel, with questions that require more than a one-word answer (for example, "What do you think will happen?" or "You seem to be angry. What's going on with you today? Can we talk about it?").

Is the Staff Skilled at Dealing with Conflict Management?

Observe how fights among the children are settled. Do the teachers scream at the preschoolers or take an authoritarian approach? Do they help the kids express their feelings and work their problems out diplomatically? Are appropriate limits set regarding the children's safety and comfort? Do the teachers follow through with consequences that make sense and are enforceable? Do they express compassion when a child is having a rough day?

If you find that these criteria are inadequately met or that the school is unreceptive to talking with you about them, we recommend that you seriously consider seeking a new placement. You are the consumer here. Everything that goes on in the preschool (including appropriate discipline, dealing with feelings, and settling fights) is part of the curriculum in which you are investing for the sake of your child.

OTHER WAYS OF CREATING SOCIAL INTERACTIONS

It's important to create social situations for your child, whether or not he is enrolled in preschool. If your child is in a day-care center, he is sure to spend time with other children. You can use the criteria we suggested above to evaluate whether the center personnel are dealing with socialization appropriately. If your child is home with you or a baby-sitter (especially if he's a first or only child), he may be more isolated. Then it is up to you to establish some kind of regular play situation that you or your sitter can attend with your child. We know from experience that finding playmates for your child is sometimes difficult.

When our older daughter was an infant and toddler, we lived in apartment buildings that were inhabited mostly by adult tenants. She had few opportunities to interact with other children on a daily basis. Outside of a five-month part-time day-care situation, she spent most of her time with her parents, grandparents, and great-grand-parents until she started preschool. In general, Susan had to made special arrangements to get together with her own friends who had children in order for Cherie to have playmates. Our daughter, consequently, felt more comfortable around adults at first than she did with children.

Cherie was three years and nine months old when Aimee was born, so our younger daughter had a built-in social situation. In addition, by the time Aimee was 18 months old we had moved into a house in a neighborhood with lots of kids (something we had looked for specifically) so that both children could have more social experiences.

Moving, of course, is a major step to take for the sake of socialization (our move met other needs as well). There are other, less drastic measures to help encourage your child's social development. Day-care placements may be ideal, as we mentioned above, as long as the care providers are sensitive and responsive to your child's needs. Mommy and Me classes as well as neighborhood play groups and co-ops sponsored by local parks, YMCA, or religious groups are great if you're not working full-time and can spare the hours during the week.

Arranging for classmates and playmates to come to your home can help to break the ice. Sleep-overs are great fun if your child is ready to handle them. At all times, an adult should be in attendance to make sure that words are used instead of fists and that toys are shared appropriately. Each time your child plays with a friend, you have a golden opportunity to teach socialization skills.

THE RIPPLE EFFECT

We stress the importance of creating a positive social environment for your preschooler as an element of kindergarten readiness because the ability to form relationships is crucial for your child's development. In fact, you may be surprised to learn that children who have problems with social skills such as working together, agreeing or disagreeing peaceably, taking turns, and sharing also have academic difficulties.

An April 1989 *Newsweek* article entitled "How Kids Learn" makes the point that "a youngster's social development has a profound effect on his academic progress. Kids who have trouble getting along with their classmates can end up behind academically as well as have a higher incidence of dropping out." They may experience difficulties adjusting to adult life, as well.

Developmentalists like Marie Winn, who wrote the book *Children Without Childhood*, have found that too much early schooling can supplant all-important playtime. This loss, in turn, has the potential of slowing or reducing a child's overall development. Usually we don't connect work and play in our minds. But for your preschooler, play *is* work. It's how he learns about his world and the people in it. For him, play—and especially social play—is not a waste of time. He really needs to play.

A family who came to see Mitch in his psychology practice illustrates how closely socialization and achievement are tied. Michael and Sandra brought in four-year-old Joshua for a consultation because he seemed listless and unhappy. They had sent him to what they felt was one of the finest schools in the city, but he complained of boredom. His teacher had scolded him on several occasions for being disruptive. The parents, at a loss to understand what was bothering their son, turned to Mitch for advice.

After a few questions, it became clear to Mitch that Joshua's school placement might be at the heart of the problem. Michael and Sandra had chosen a very small nursery school, one in which the student-teacher ratio was about eight-to-one. They figured, and rightly so, that Joshua would get a lot of individualized attention from the teacher in such an exclusive setting. He also received a good deal of reading-readiness instruction, which pleased them. The school, however, didn't meet Josh's social needs. He found his seven classmates uninteresting, and there were not enough kids his age for him to choose from in making friends.

Even though Josh was to begin kindergarten in only nine months, Mitch suggested that Michael and Sandra explore changing his preschool. After some soul-searching and a good deal of research, they made the switch to a much larger school. What a difference it made in Josh's attitude! He was thrilled to have the ability to pick and choose among potential friends, and he seemed to be learning more readily and more happily. When there's a lot of socialization going on, children learn from each other.

WHEN KIDS HAVE SOCIAL PROBLEMS

The ideal situation is one in which your child feels loved and accepted by friends all the time. This is an impossibility, however. No matter how socially competent, all children (as well as all adults) feel rejection once in a while.

According to a recent *New York Times* article by columnist Lawrence Kutner entitled "The Best Way to Help Rejected Children Gain Acceptance Is to Teach Them New Social Skills," research shows that occasional rejection by classmates is nothing to worry about. Children who are teased or ignored for several months at a time, however, require some help from their parents and preschool teacher.

Dr. Steven R. Ascher, director of the Bureau of Educational Research at the University of Illinois at Champaign-Urbana, was quoted in the article as saying, "The children who are rejected may be aggressive, or they may be apprehensive and submissive. The common denominator is the lack of positive social skills such as how to initiate and maintain relationships or how to resolve conflicts with other children."

The most common way of dealing with these problems is to teach children the skills they are lacking, such as how to

★ share
★ wait their turn
★ play games according to the rules
★ respond to teasing
★ put their feelings into words

How can you teach these skills? Many children learn about cooperation and sharing from the incidents portrayed on public television's "Sesame Street." From the shows we watched years ago we remember a segment, for example, in which three Muppets were hungry. One had peanut butter, the second had bread, and the third had a bottle of milk. They decided to cooperate so that they all got what they wanted—peanut butter sandwiches and a glass of milk.

Another of our favorites was a scene in which Bert and Ernie tried to share two pieces of licorice whip candy. Ernie, ever the wise guy, kept taking bites of candy to even up the score. Each time he chomped on Bert's licorice, he took too much and so had to eat more of his own—until he had eaten it all, to Bert's utter exasperation.

Such scenes on "Sesame Street" can spark conversations between you and your preschooler about his interactions with others. You can also teach socialization skills by your positive example and by talking to your child once a particular situation arises, as in the beach incident we mentioned earlier. Expressions like the following can help teach social interaction skills.

★ "It's important to share. Let Allison play with the doll now. You'll get it back later."
★ "I understand that you're angry, but it's never OK to hit. Use your words."
★ "No one else is pushing on this line. See, everyone has to wait his turn and you do, too."
★ "Don't just run away and hide. If Anthony hurt your feelings, you need to let him know. Come on, let's go talk to him."
★ "It's not OK to take someone else's things. Put it back."

WHAT IF YOUR CHILD IS AGGRESSIVE?

In terms of social skills, it seems an ounce of prevention is worth a ton of cure. It's hard for children to change their opinions of their peers once negative reputations have been firmly established.

In one research study reported in the *New York Times* article mentioned above, older children were told a story in which a classmate did something bad to them. When the incident involved someone they liked, they responded that the child didn't really mean to act badly. If, on the other hand, it involved a child they did not like, the children responded, "He's always doing that to be mean. He's always mean." The behavior in the two stories was exactly the same.

It's no fun being labeled the mean one in the crowd. Children who are aggressive are often ostracized from their peer group. Who wants to play with a bully? Most often, aggressive children lack socialization skills. They haven't learned to put their feelings into words. When they are upset, they strike out at the nearest target. This may be the person who angered them, but if that person is an adult or a threatening figure, their anger may be redirected at another child or a pet.

It's important to bear in mind that anger in itself is neither bad nor good. It is an emotion like any other emotion. As Mitch wrote in his parent-child manual, *Sometimes It's OK to Be Angry!:*

> It is difficult for children to make the distinction between the emotion of anger and what is done with the anger. To a child, they are one and the same. . . . If we are to separate the two in the child's mind, we parents must communicate the difference. We can teach a child that he or she can feel angry and express that anger, yet not be destructive. In other words, it is OK to be angry, but it is not OK to behave in a destructive manner out of anger.

What your child *does* with his anger is the question here. It's perfectly fine for your preschooler to be angry, but it's not acceptable for him to hurt himself or others or to destroy property.

Children learn aggressive behavior. They pick it up from siblings, parents, neighborhood children, and preschool playmates. By the same token, they can also learn to put their feelings into words.

If you find that your preschooler is acting aggressively, you might want to help him identify his feelings and channel them more constructively. For example, you can say, "I understand that you're unhappy about your new sister, but it's not OK to poke at her. Here, why don't you take out your angry feelings on this doll? Let's pretend the doll is your sister." Other activities can also release angry tension appropriately: running; hitting a ball, a pile of pillows, or a punching bag with all of one's might; or playing with clay.

If your child continues to hit, pinch, bite, or carry on in other hurtful or inappropriate ways, you must assert suitable discipline. In this case, you must create a limit (such as, "No fighting!"); establish a consequence ("If you continue to hit Mary, I will have to separate you"); and then follow through appropriately when the limit is tested (for it surely will be). That means being consistent. Each and every time that your child fights with her friend, insist that she take a time-out (five to ten boring minutes alone in her room) to think about what she has done. If she knows that you mean business, eventually her behavior will improve, and she will benefit from her improved socialization skills.

WHAT ABOUT SHYNESS?

There is a difference between a withdrawn child and one who is just shy. Usually, the former has suffered some trauma or loss, such as a death or divorce in the family; some sort of physical, emotional, or sexual abuse; or placement in foster care. In these cases, withdrawal is often a sign of childhood depression. (Interestingly, some children withdraw under these circumstances while others act out their anger and become aggressive.) Withdrawn children lose interest in their favorite activities and toys. They pull back from any social contact. This is a relatively severe situation that warrants the intervention of a trained child counselor.

Shyness, on the other hand, is an emotion that can be a normal part of childhood. In Mitch's parent-child manual, *It's OK to Be Shy!*, he explains that some preschoolers are shy around other children because they lack social skills. They may have been surrounded almost exclusively by adults (as our older daughter was), or they may not have been prepared for a new situation. It's normal for children to be reticent at first when thrust into a new setting with unfamiliar people. Shyness can be a product of lack of experience with the unfamiliar.

The best way to help your child with shyness is first *not* to label her behavior. Kids have a way of living up (or down) to your expectations of them. If you're always explaining to friends that Jennifer is shy, then, by golly, she's going to believe that she is and she's going to act that way. It becomes a self-fulfilling prophecy. Labeling may help you explain your daughter's behavior, but it also pigeonholes her so that she can't explore new avenues of interaction.

In addition, your preschooler may sense that you're upset about her shy behavior. Jennifer may use this information to get what she wants from you. Every time she wants attention, she may act shy. Usually the best way to deal with this situation is to ignore the behavior. If you do so consistently, it will often go away.

If your child is truly and painfully uncomfortable around other children or new situations, however, there are ways you can help her overcome her reticence.

Explain What's Going to Happen

Situations and people won't seem so unfamiliar if you've spent some time preparing your preschooler about what to expect. For example, if you're going to visit some friends with preschoolers whom Robin hasn't yet met, you can explain to her that David and Brian are four and five years old and that they love to play with trucks and Masters of the Universe characters. Of course, you can't foresee all possibilities, but Robin will have an idea of who and what to expect. This may ease her apprehensiveness.

Try Lots of New Situations

If your child feels unhappy and awkward in unfamiliar surroundings, you may feel inclined to shun these in order to reduce her discomfort. After all, if she's unhappy, why make things worse?

Such a solution may be shortsighted, however. In truth, life is filled with new situations that we all must deal with. We change schools or jobs with some regularity, we move to new living quarters from time to time, we try new supermarkets and shopping malls. If you keep your child at home all the time so that she won't feel uncomfortable, she may have a harder time adjusting to the natural variations that occur in the rhythm of life.

It is advisable, rather, to expose her to new situations. This can be done slowly and gently. You don't have to take her to the circus the first time out, but you can try a new playground or a new friend's home. The more variety she is exposed to, the less frightening new situations will eventually become.

Get Your Child Involved in New Activities

Children who have a hard time making friends often come together during fun activities. Signing up for swimming, tumbling, or arts and crafts at the local park or YMCA can be a giant step toward overcoming shyness. Just make sure to follow your child's interests. The benefits are twofold. Not only will your child learn new skills, but somehow she will experience the activity as a bridge. Once children become engaged in the doing of a project, they are able to let go of their fears. They interact with their playmates and emerge from their shells.

PUTTING IT ALL INTO PERSPECTIVE

As you can see, your child's social skills are essential for his success in kindergarten and thereafter. But school alone can't be responsible for all of the subtle interactions that occur among people in your preschooler's world from day to day. Therefore you as parents should put as much effort into teaching about relationships as you do reading readiness. The "flashcards" of socialization are cooperation, sharing, and putting feelings into words. Everyday situations in your child's life will give you many opportunities to teach these essential skills.

CHAPTER 5

Early Reading:
You Can't Hurry Love . . . or Readiness

A lot has been said and written about early reading. While many parents are eager to have their children get a head start, most experts feel that early reading is essentially a waste of time. They contend that children who learn to read early do so because their parents pressure them or because it's a way to gain attention from adults who are otherwise too preoccupied. In fact, some say that to push a child into reading before he is ready can be detrimental; the preschooler will be turned off and may not want to read later.

We tend to agree with this point of view. We hope the previous chapters have made it clear that your preschooler's ability to form relationships rather than his academic achievement is the solid basis of kindergarten readiness. Besides, it's impossible to hurry your child's maturation. As Fritz Perls, the Gestalt psychologist of the '60s, used to say in other contexts, "Don't push the river. It flows by itself."

In fact, such an attempt is a waste of everyone's time. You may end up angry, while your preschooler may feel inadequate in his frustrated attempts to achieve goals that you've set for him. This can impair his pleasure in learning and his feelings of self-worth. You will accomplish just the opposite of what you've set out to do.

The truth is, children get "ready" to read when they're good and ready. Some may be eager to read when they are four years old; others only catch the reading bug at six and a half. Each child's needs should be met individually. Despite your anxiety about reading, most studies show that by the time children reach the second grade, most have mastered the skill.

EARLY AND "LATE" READING IN OUR FAMILY

We've had both positive and negative experiences with early reading in our family. Our older daughter, Cherie, was highly motivated to read, and she caught on quickly. She began recognizing words like "STOP" on the traffic sign and "milk" on the carton at about three. She seemed to understand that these funny written symbols actually represented what cars had to do and the white stuff that she drank. She watched "Sesame Street" and "Electric Company" ad nauseum and repeated the letters and words as they flashed on the screen.

At that time, Mitch was a reading specialist enrolled in a master's program in education and Susan was a French literature student. There was no lack of books in the house. Mitch bought workbooks for Cherie to play with. Reading was a natural experience—it was what everyone seemed to be doing in the house a lot of the time. Cherie truly seemed motivated and interested.

Contrary to the assessments of the experts, Cherie's early interest grew into a love for the written word. In the first grade, she acted as a peer tutor in reading for kindergarten kids. By the second grade, she took a class in the "great books." Her teacher placed her in a fifth-grade classroom's reading lesson daily because she was functioning well at that level.

As Cherie got older, she grew to love reading series of books, which she seemed to digest whole and then reread forever. She went through the *Black Stallion* series, the *Little House* series, and the *Chronicles of Narnia,* to name a few. From these she seemed to find symbols that helped her to make sense of the world. She acted out the stories in her playtimes with her friends.

Aimee, on the other hand, was more interested in purely social play activities than in reading. Hers was the more usual developmental pattern. Susan, however, mistakenly assumed that both children would be on the same wavelength and tried to teach four-year-old Aimee to read. As you can expect, this just didn't work. Aimee, a bit young for her grade anyway, wasn't much interested in sitting still and reading *Hop on Pop, Pup in Cup,* or *Sis in a Mess.* A power struggle developed between mother and daughter, Susan fervently believing that Aimee could read if only she gave it a try, and Aimee letting her know in no uncertain terms that she wasn't interested.

It may not surprise you to learn that Aimee has no great fondness for reading to this day. She tolerates books when given assignments, and we must admit that she did shed a tear when she read *Little Women* and she enjoyed *To Kill a Mockingbird* once she got involved in it. Given a full afternoon with absolutely nothing to do, however, you will not find her curling up in a comfortable chair with a book on her lap.

Should we trace Aimee's reluctance to read back to her negative preschool experiences with her mother? We could. But it's also possible that her interests and abilities simply lie in different areas. She has tremendous social and athletic skills. She made the varsity softball team, for example, in the tenth grade. She has artistic and dramatic talents, as well. She shares few of these affinities with her big sister.

This brings us to two other points. First, there are many different types of intelligence. We are shortsighted if we consider reading as the only criterion for judging a child's future success. Second, kids will grow and flourish, sometimes because of our best efforts and sometimes—disconcertingly so—despite them. Aimee had a particular need to be different from Cherie. She wanted to be her own person. If that meant not being a super reader, then so be it.

As you can see, we had mixed results from our homegrown reading-readiness efforts. These results depended more on our children's interests and personalities than on our "teaching." It's important to take your cues from your children and not push them into reading as a way to please you.

Some parents don't feel competent to teach reading readiness themselves. They trust the preschool to do the job for them. Should you rely on your preschool to provide formal reading instruction? That depends on how the teacher goes about it. Let's backtrack for a moment to understand why.

A CAUTIONARY TALE ABOUT
PRESCHOOL READING READINESS

When Cherie was about three, we moved from one part of Los Angeles to another. Our new home was too far from her original preschool to commute, so we had to seek out a new placement.

Cherie's first nursery school was a sweet and gentle place. Her teacher, Mrs. Tucker, had recognized Cherie's love for koala bears and made a special effort to find books and stories that included the cute, furry marsupials from Australia. Mrs. Tucker also recognized that Cherie was extraordinarily verbal. She encouraged us to read and converse with our daughter as much as possible.

When we set out to look for a new nursery school, Susan thought it might be a good idea to find one that stressed reading readiness. After all, she reasoned, Cherie was very bright and precocious. She already recognized some letters and sounds. Wouldn't it be great if she got a head start on reading? Just think of the possibilities.

Susan hauled out the Yellow Pages and started calling preschools in the vicinity to get an idea of their orientation. She found one that sounded ideal. The director explained that the children had forty-five minutes of reading-readiness instruction daily. He boasted about the school's structured academic program.

Excited by the prospect of giving Cherie that extra push (this was seventeen years ago—long before the current trend to hurry children's education), Susan made an appointment to observe the class with our daughter the next day. When they arrived, just in time for reading instruction, they were ushered into a large, clean class-room. About twelve three-year-olds were seated in a semicricle around the teacher and her chalkboard.

After less than ten minutes of "instruction," Susan began to feel the tension among the children. It was an almost palpable sensation. Three of the kids wiggled and jiggled as if they needed to use the bathroom something fierce. One girl twirled her hair, sucked her thumb, and stared off into space. Two little boys jumped out of their chairs and took off around the circumference of the circle, screaming as they went. The teacher quieted them down, but after another minute or so they were in orbit again. The rest of the kids seemed restless and unhappy.

Cherie, in the meantime, hung on to the edges of her seat and rocked herself back and forth, as if restraining herself from getting up and leaving. The teacher was now on the verge of shouting at the class in order to maintain a semblance of order for the visitors. By the time the "lesson" was over thirty-five very long minutes later, Susan had a crashing headache and Cherie suffered from terminal crabbiness.

The day was not a total loss. Susan had learned a very impor-tant—albeit inadvertent—lesson herself. Despite fads and fashions in education, preschool is not the time to engage in formal reading instruction. That has to come later, as children develop abstract reasoning and other intellectual skills as well as a long enough attention span.

Preschool is the time for children to learn about the world around them through active exploration, movement, and manipulative and fantasy play. It's when kids learn how to interact with other children. Reading readiness—at least in a formal classroom environment—has to wait.

WHY THOSE KIDS JUST COULDN'T SIT STILL

As it turned out, Susan's instincts were right on target. The April 1989 feature article in *Newsweek*, "How Kids Learn," focuses on the importance of exploration and play in child development and learning. The article quotes (among other experts) Dr. Martha Denckla, professor of neurology and pediatrics at Johns Hopkins University. According to Dr. Denckla, "A young child has to make a conscious effort to sit still. A large chunk of children can't do it. It's a very energy-consuming activity for them."

The article makes the point that small children actually get more tired when they have to sit still and listen than when they have the freedom to move around the room. Apparently the part of the brain that controls a child's natural curiosity and energy, the frontal lobe, is still immature in some children until the age of nine. As the lobe develops so does the child's ability to tolerate boredom. Your preschooler, of course, doesn't have a clue about how to be attentive to a lecture.

To expect a group of three- and four-year-olds to be able to sit still enough to learn a reading "lesson," therefore, is not only ill-advised, it is also developmentally inappropriate and perhaps even emotionally damaging. Kids don't do well when demands are made of them that they can never fulfill. No matter how well intentioned, schools and parents that put too much pressure on children to perform tasks for which they are not developmentally equipped can exert negative effects. According to Tufts University psychologist Dr. David Elkind, child-advocate and author of *The Hurried Child: Growing Up Too Fast Too Soon* and *Miseducation: Preschoolers at Risk*, school itself can be treacherous:

> The child's budding sense of competence is frequently under attack, not only from inappropriate instructional practices . . . but also from the hundred and one feelings of hurt, frustration and rejection

that mark a child's entrance into the world of schooling, competition and peer-group involvement.

Adults can rationalize their frustrations or gain some perspective by comparing current problems to past successes. If you lost out on a sale today, for example, you can remember the deals you struck last week and the week before that were so lucrative. You trust that in the future you will succeed again. Young children don't have these experiences or inner resources to fall back on. They may begin to feel as if they're failures early in their educational careers—especially if they don't fulfill parents' expectations that they read, for example, by the age of four or five.

Why are we telling you this? Because we want to allay your fears that your child is not ready to read at this point. Even if she shows a proclivity to reading, like our older daughter did by learning the alphabet early, it's better to stress other areas first. Think of it this way: If you've just recently mastered running one lap around the track, would you attempt to enter the Boston Marathon? A quarter mile does not a long-distance runner make. Likewise, you'll want to develop an interest and enthusiasm for reading in your preschooler without pushing the actual skills for which she may still be immature.

Can you expect your child to learn *anything* about reading in preparation for kindergarten? Of course. But it's not just what she learns, it's how it's taught that's significant. Reading-readiness activities should not be carried out with blackboard and chalk or workbooks and pencils. They should be fun group activities that engage children in interacting with one another.

What your preschooler should be learning during her preschool reading experience is that reading is a pleasurable activity—one that she would love to engage in.

CREATING ENTHUSIASM FOR READING

In terms of reading readiness, your role should be to encourage your child's interest, enjoyment, and motivation. These are the keys to readiness. Here are some strategies you may find helpful. Some of these fine suggestions we've adapted from Margery Kranyik's book *Starting School.*

Make Story Time a Fun Time

Set aside ten to fifteen minutes daily for stories. Make sure you're not interrupted—this is special time. Cuddle up together. Put your arm around your child. Story time should be a special part of the day when you share warmth and love. No pressure on the child, please.

Engage Your Child in the Story

Sometimes we get so caught up in achievement, we forget that interactions are important, too. Rather than fixing your sights on the end of the story, you may want to just meander through it. Have your child look at the pictures and make up a story to go with them. This motivates him and activates his imagination. You might stop when you get to a high point and ask your preschooler what he thinks is going to happen next. You may not finish the tale, but so what? Your goal here is to help him think and make choices. You're not in a race to the finish.

Read with Your Preschooler Rather than to Him

Encourage his questions and comments. The process may be more important than the content. Even if he interrupts, he is connecting to the story and to you. His ability to put his ideas into words is an important part of school readiness, as we'll see in the next chapter.

Tape-record or Videotape Yourself
Reading Your Child's Favorite Stories

You can add your own sound effects and comments. Then, when you're not available to read to him, your preschooler can leaf through the book and follow the story. He'll feel close to you, too.

Keep a Wide Variety of Reading Materials

We used to order *Sesame Street Magazine* for our kids when they were preschoolers. It was always exciting for them to receive their own mail, and the magazine reinforced what they had seen on TV. They loved doing the puzzles as well. As they grew older, we subscribed to other publications, like *World*, published for children by the National Geographic Society. It's also important to have other types of reading material on hand such as books of poetry, nursery rhymes, alphabet rhymes, and counting games.

Refer to the Newspaper

You can read short human interest stories to your child from the paper. Show him the pictures. Look at the advertisements and the comics. This helps preschoolers learn that reading is not some abstract idea but concretely connects them to their world.

Read Labels on Boxes and Jars

We used to point out common words on household items. That's how our daughter recognized the word "milk" on the carton. Eventually these become *sight words*—words the preschooler can identify on sight without having to sound them out.

Take Frequent Trips to the Library

Susan remembers library day in her childhood as a time of great anticipation, a chance to satisfy her nearly insatiable curiosity. Before our kids could even walk, she began making regular trips to the library with them so that they also could acquire a love of learning. Susan even found some of her own old favorites in the shelves among the newer children's books. What a thrill it was to read these to our kids.

Set a Good Example

Your child will believe that reading is worthwhile if he observes you in that activity daily. Read the newspaper, magazines, or a book.

THE LARGER PICTURE

We hope this chapter has helped you to put your preschooler's reading readiness in some sort of perspective. It's helpful to keep in mind that what appears today as a deficiency may tomorrow turn out to be a valuable asset, and vice versa. We may think that reading at four years old is a desirable goal, but in fact it may be more detrimental than helpful. Conversely, we may be upset about our preschooler's lack of interest in the written word, but he may be quite busy developing other parts of his personality as he gets ready to tackle books with greater confidence later on.

This reminds us of an old Sufi tale about a wealthy farmer, Amad, whose prized Arabian stallion ran away. His neighbor came to him and said, "Amad, how terrible! You have lost your best horse."

Amad replied, "Maybe."

The following day, the horse returned, bringing two mares along. Now his neighbor said, "Amad, how wonderful! Now you have three horses instead of one. Perhaps you will have colts, soon, too."

Amad replied, "Maybe."

The following day, Amad's son jumped on the back of one of the mares and rode it around the farm. Before long a big wind came along and frightened the steed. It reared back and threw the boy to the ground, and he broke his arm. Now the neighbor said, "Amad, how terrible. Your only son has broken his arm. How will he help you to gather the crops? This is truly a catastrophe."

Amad replied, "Maybe."

The next day, the army rode through the countryside, looking for conscripts for their next battle. They came to Amad's farm, having heard that he had a young son whom they could spirit away. But when they saw the son's broken arm, they left him behind to seek someone else who was more fit. Now Amad's neighbor was beside himself with excitement at his friend's good fortune. Amad's measured reply was still, "Maybe."

None of us can fully assess the impact of decisions on our children's futures. As the parents of high school and college-age children, only now can we look back on courses of action abandoned or adopted and evaluate where we made mistakes or were successful. As parents, you can do no more. All of us can only hope to do our best in the moment—for that's all we have.

CHAPTER 6

The Three Cs of Kindergarten Readiness: Encouraging Curiosity, Conversation, and Creativity

Your preschooler's curiosity, her ability to carry on conversations, and her creativity are the keys to her future love of learning and to her development as a whole person. We like to call these the three Cs of kindergarten readiness. All three attributes are essential to your child's educational future. They involve the manipulation of *ideas*.

The curious child is willing to explore uncharted seas in her quest for understanding. She wants to fathom the way the world works. The child who has good conversation skills is able to clearly express her ideas to others, and she can in turn benefit from the give-and-take that dialogue provides. The creative child has lots of ideas of her own which she may express verbally or through art, dance, scientific inquiry, writing (eventually), or other media. When you encourage all three of the Cs in your child—watch out! The sky can be the limit.

In truth, the academic skills a child picks up during her preschool years can pale in comparison to the importance of a sharpened curiosity, the ability to express ideas, and a sense of exploration and creativity. These latter will serve her well beyond the kindergarten experience. In fact, they (along with a dogged persistence) may form the cornerstones to success throughout elementary school, high school, college, and in the world beyond.

In the course of this chapter, we will cover each of the three Cs in more detail and provide you with strategies to augment your child's love of learning by enhancing them. By no means should you limit yourself to our suggestions. Let these be a jumping-off point for your own creative ideas.

CURIOSITY *CAN* KILL THE CAT

As we mentioned in the previous chapter, Susan was an endlessly curious child. Her family's folklore is replete with tales of her antics. There was the time she took apart her radio because she wanted to see who was talking in there. Of course, she had no idea how to reassemble the pile of parts, once she had discovered that radio transmissions came from some mysterious force beyond her comprehension.

Then there was the time she buried her gloves in the snow at the schoolyard to see if she could find them. After two readily successful trials, she decided the challenge was too easy, so on the third attempt she circled the playground several times with her eyes closed before trying to locate the hidden treasure. Need we say more? She came home with cold hands and a red face that day.

But everyone's favorite was the staple story. This was no ordinary staple, mind you, but a heavy-duty industrial-strength tin fastener, the kind that gets shot out of a staple gun at forty miles per hour. Susan had found this gem on the floor of her great-aunt's dry-goods store on a visit there. In natural four-year-old fashion, Susan wanted to know how far she could push it up her nose. She found, much to her amazement and consternation, that she could get it up quite far—so much so that she couldn't retrieve it with her finger.

Rather than tell her mom about her experiment—heaven forbid—Susan thought she'd wait it out. Once cousins, aunts, uncles, parents, and sister were assembled around the dinner table, Susan's nose decided that it had had enough of the foreign body. It gave a mighty sneeze and the staple flew from its resting place, making a loud "plink" as it landed on the floor.

"What was that?" demanded Susan's rather astonished mother in front of the assembled family. We leave it to you to imagine the rest of the story.

This all goes to show that curiosity can sometimes kill the cat. Kids can get into the most outrageous predicaments when they follow the famous lure, "What if . . .?" In a recent *Calvin and Hobbes* cartoon, for example, Calvin got into a heap of trouble because he wanted to see if he could push his mom's car out of the garage just a little bit. He never accounted for the force of gravity interacting with the slant of the driveway and the heft of the car.

None of this is to say that curiosity is a negative trait. As Susan and her co-author Dr. Susan Ludington-Hoe have written in their book *How to Have a Smarter Baby*, "You *do* want your [child] to be curious. A curious person asks the question, 'What if . . . ?' He wants to know more, to dig for new insights and information. A curious person is very bright. The more he knows, the more he wants to know. He is always looking for *new* knowledge."

We would have to say that the same holds true for Susan today. In writing books she has become a perennial student, perpetually in search of new information. In a similar vein, curiosity can be a valuable component of your child's readiness for kindergarten. It constitutes part of an all-important attribute—the love of learning.

QUALITY TIME—IN QUANTITY—
TO ENCOURAGE CURIOSITY

"Quality time" was all the rage several years ago. Many of us came to believe that we didn't have to spend much time with our kids as long as the time was well spent. While it's true that what's important is not just the minutes but the interaction that occurs during those minutes (for example, a half hour of dozing next to your son while he's watching "Pee-wee's Playhouse" does *not* constitute quality time), it is also true that the more time spent together the better. Even if your child is in a top-flight preschool, he still needs contact with you. Five minutes each evening can't substitute for an hour. Quantities of quality time are the best.

Quality time means paying attention to the kinds of interactions that occur during your moments with your preschooler. Are you simply filling the time with "approved" activities? Or do the activities work toward building your relationship and your child's inquisitiveness? As you may have guessed, we feel the latter is the ideal. For example, parents frequently exert a lot of energy in the *buying* of toys. Too often most of the excitement is expended on the way to the toy store; the quality interactions occur in the store rather than in exploring the new objects. By the time you get home, you're all too tired to enjoy the toys.

To remedy this situation, how about organizing a lending library of toys and games with friends, family, and neighbors? Not only will you save money but you will also spend more time actually playing with the toys rather than acquiring them, and your kids will be exposed to a wider variety of playthings than they normally would.

Sometimes improvised playthings provide more fun than purchased toys. The large box from your new washer, for example, can set the stage for hours of creative play. Together you can paint the outside of the box and decorate it within to resemble a playhouse, rocketship, classroom, or car. The possibilities are limitless.

How can you encourage curiosity during your time together? Preschoolers have a refreshing and innocent sense of wonder about the world. They experience their environment as a mystery. To them, everything is new and exciting. Since they are learning about the world around them, nature activities seem an ideal vehicle for kindling curiosity.

You can spend your time together planting carrots, radishes, or marigold seeds—even if your garden is only a large Styrofoam cup with a hole punched in the bottom, placed in the sunlight on a windowsill. Talk to your child about the growth cycle and how seeds need sun, water, and nutrients from the soil in order to flourish. Have her water the seedlings and watch as they sprout into mature plants. Let her experience the wonder of eating her homegrown vegetables or witnessing the opening and eventual death of a flower. Harvest seeds for the next crop.

As you're engaged in this activity, ask plenty of questions like, "What do you think would happen if . . . ?" You might even set up a tiny science experiment, contrasting seeds that were watered versus those that were not, or plants left in the sun versus others placed in a closet.

You might help your preschooler build a nest for a caterpillar she has found on the sidewalk. Rather than shouting "Yuck!" and squashing the green furry critter underfoot, help her line a small plastic container or jar with leaves and flower petals and sprinkle some water inside it. Add a sturdy twig. Cover the container with plastic wrap with several air holes poked in it and secure it with a rubber band. You may be lucky enough to find a cocoon hanging from the twig several days later. Eventually a butterfly may emerge. Talk with your preschooler about the miraculous transformation you have both observed, and then set the butterfly free.

Finally, quality time often means engaging in conversation with your child about the activities you have undertaken. When you walk to the market, for example, you can pay attention to and talk about the different flowers in neighbors' gardens, the various colors of grass, the breeds of large and small dogs that charge at you from behind gates, the makes of cars, the types of businesses along the way. When you're making meatballs, you can discuss the ingredients and the consistency of the food.

As you engage in these activities, make sure that you ask plenty of questions: "Why do you think this lawn is so yellow and that one so green?" "That's a pet store. What kinds of animals do you think are in there? Do you think we'll find some dinosaurs? Why not? Let's take a look inside." Such conversations help to increase your preschooler's vocabulary, enrich his thought processes, and spark his own curiosity about the world around him. When you merely hurry through your tasks, you both miss out on so much.

THE SECOND C: CONVERSATION

Conversations to pique your preschooler's natural curiosity are part of a broader issue: the necessity for you to talk with your child frequently so that she learns to express her own complex ideas.

When we began writing this book, we contacted Aimee's former kindergarten teacher, Arla Capps. We have remained friends with Arla all these years and we felt that as an excellent teacher, her perspective was valuable. When Susan asked Arla what she felt parents most needed to do in preparing their children for kindergarten, she replied without hesitation and with some vehemence, "Conversation! Children just aren't being listened to these days. They should be encouraged to speak in sentences by parents who listen to what they have to say. Parents should answer their children's questions and engage them in real conversations."

In her experience, Arla has found that many entering kindergarteners have a hard time expressing themselves. Language development is enhanced when preschoolers are allowed to struggle through complex thoughts, she explains. "Children should be encouraged to try to repeat what they've just seen. If you've just come back from a trip to the doctor or supermarket, let them talk about it. They need to be given the chance to express themselves. Yet, more often than not, kids are just commanded at. Parents order them around instead of asking them what they think.

"When kids don't have the opportunity to use language," Arla continues, "they can't recognize basic words. If a child has never heard or used the word 'ceiling,' for example, he won't be able to read it."

Arla places some of the blame for poor language development on television. "In many families, TV raises the kids. The babysitter may plunk the child down in front of the set to keep him quiet. But when a child watches a lot of television, he is talked to without being given the opportunity to answer. He never learns to formulate what's on his mind. He becomes very passive in the use of language."

How would Arla correct this situation? Obviously, she believes that talking to your child is important. But, she says, questions need to be directed. "If you pick your son up from preschool and ask him, 'Did you get to play with the paints today?' you're only going to get a yes or no answer." That's not good enough. Instead, she recommends asking open-ended questions, like "What did you paint today?" or "How did you and Jeffrey get along?"

If your child still gives you only monosyllabic answers, pursue your line of questioning further. For example, if he answers, "A tree" to your first question about painting, you can follow up with:

★ "Why did you choose a tree?"

★ "What color did you paint it?"

★ "What did it look like?"

★ "Was it a maple, an oak, or a sycamore?" (This question, of course, could engender a long conversation about these different trees and their attributes.)

★ "How many branches did it have?"

★ "How is it the same as or different from the tree in front of our apartment building?"

★ "What did your teacher say when she saw it?"

Often when we retrieve our kids from preschool, our minds are still caught up in the trials and tribulations of work. We ride home in silence. Conversations such as the one Arla suggests can help us make the transition from work to home more smoothly. To this day, when Susan picks up Aimee from high school, they have a detailed talk in the car about how their day went and what they did. It's a nice way to connect.

GETTING YOUR CHILD TO CONVERSE

The following suggestions have helped us have fruitful conversations with our children, ones in which they have felt valued and listened to. You may not be able to incorporate all of these ideas into your conversations at once, but you can work at including them as time goes on.

Get Down to Your Child's Level

In parenting classes, Mitch often carries out an experiment. He stands on a chair and lectures to the people attending the workshop from this perch. After a few minutes he surveys the group, and invariably the adults complain of strained backs and craned necks. Your preschooler has to put up with this disadvantage in size all the time. When you want to talk, it's best for you to sit down or have him join you at your height by standing on a safe stool or chair. When our daughters wanted to participate in cookie baking, for example, they climbed on a chair so they were counter- and mommy-height.

Really Listen

We all have lots of things on our minds. As parents in today's world, we feel pressured by our hectic lives. However, when your preschooler speaks to you and you answer distractedly, absent-mindedly, or even not at all, he will learn that what he has to say isn't really very important to you. If it's not important to his parents—the most significant people in his life—then certainly others won't be interested either. He may withdraw and stop talking.

A child who is listened to feels cared about and valued. Your simple act of listening carefully and responding appropriately serves to increase your preschooler's self-esteem.

Make Eye Contact

The eyes have been called the windows of the soul. Many emotions, especially love, are expressed through the eyes. Your preschooler understands these nonverbal cues even from birth. When you look into your child's eyes as you speak, you are letting him know that all of your attention is focused on him. He learns that his eyes are a valuable tool for communication with others, as well.

Speak in Sentences

One of the best ways of encouraging your preschooler to express complex ideas is to get him used to complex ideas in the first place. Monosyllabic answers and grunts and groans from you will elicit the same from him. Speak in sentences, and use open-ended questions to prompt longer replies from your child.

Use Puppets

Sometimes children have a hard time expressing themselves to adults but find hand and finger puppets easier to relate to. Child psychologists know that puppets help to stimulate children's language development by exciting their imagination. You can act out a story using puppets and have your preschooler respond. You might encourage him to make his own puppet show for your enjoyment.

Don't Make It Easy for Him

Often second- and third-born children have their needs attended to by older siblings who respond to pointing fingers and whines. If your younger child learns that he can get what he wants without having to say it, he'll take the easy way out. In that case, we recommend that you not respond until your child tells you *in words* what he's after. Don't play guessing games or put words in his mouth. Encourage your older children to respond only when the younger child expresses himself verbally. He may not like this approach and may even throw a tantrum, but it's essential for his language development. Hang in there.

When your preschooler gets accustomed to using conversation, he enjoys multiple benefits. He learns that he can ask for what he wants, and thus he reduces his aggressive behavior. He expresses his ideas and curiosity about the world. Most important, he feels loved and valued.

FAMILY ACTIVITIES TO TALK ABOUT

Now that you know how to communicate, what are you going to talk about? One of the easiest ways to carry on a conversation with your preschooler is to have a ready topic. Stories are ideal. As we discussed in the previous chapter, when you stop and talk about what you're reading and ask questions like, "What do you think will happen next?" you can initiate wonderful conversations with your preschooler.

In addition, sharing a variety of new experiences often provides rich topics of conversation. As an extra benefit, your child's natural curiosity and imagination will be piqued by some of the following outings:

airport
amusement park
art museum
ball game or other sporting event
beach
children's museum
circus or ice show
concerts, ballets, or plays (especially those geared for children)
department store
downtown (if you live in the suburbs)
farm or countryside (if you're a city-dweller)
grandma's house
movies
natural history museum
park
planetarium
puppet or marionette show
zoo

All of these experiences provide topics for discussion. At the beach, for example:

★ You can talk about the size of the waves and the coldness of the water. *"Where do you think waves come from, anyway?"*

★ You can dig for sand crabs. *"Will they survive in the bucket of water? How about on the hot, dry sand?"*

★ You can erect monumental sand castles, discussing turrets, moats, and drawbridges. *"Did you know that kings and queens used to live in big castles like these? What do you think their lives were like?"*

★ You can observe and comment on other families at rest and at play. The beach is a great laboratory for studying human behavior. *"Why do you think that little girl is crying?"*

★ You can cover a bit of geography (*"Do you think we can dig to China?"*), marine biology (*"What if we pop the air bubbles in the seaweed?"*), or geology (*"Can we bury Dad in the sand?"*).

★ Most of all, you can impart to your child a sense of wonder at the vastness of the Earth and universe and her place in the great scheme of things.

Just remember, for everyone's utmost enjoyment, to keep your activities with your preschooler short and sweet. In our book *Disciplining Your Preschooler and Feeling Good About It*, we cover this subject at length. Limiting the timing of activities has to do with your own expectations. You won't get the most out of a trip to the zoo, for example, if your preschooler is tired and cranky. Here is what we recommended:

> If we decided to go to the zoo, we usually did not make an afternoon of it. Instead, we would arrive early in the morning and spend only about an hour looking at perhaps the elephants, zebras, giraffes, monkeys, and rhinoceroses. And then we would go home. On the next trip, maybe the following month, we would see the lions, tigers, snakes, and birds. . . . In that way, the kids didn't become bored or overtired as a result of *our* longer attention spans or our adult need to see it all.

As your child gets older, you can add sections of the zoo or museum to your itinerary. In the meantime, keep in mind that you won't get in much fruitful conversation if you're dragging a crabby or screaming child around the zoo.

THE MANY FACES OF THE THIRD C: CREATIVITY

Creativity is not easily defined. It can take innumerable forms. In fact, each person's imagination is as unique as his fingerprints—no two minds are alike.

Children often express their creativity during conversations with you. Preschoolers, especially, love to tell tall tales. Kids also use language in new and unique ways. Mitch, for example, remembers a talk he had with Jonathan, a little boy who put his hand on his *ears* because he was starving.

"Why are you doing that?" Mitch asked.

"I'm so hungry," Jonathan answered. "I don't want my ears to hear how hungry I am because then I'll get even hungrier." We'll bet not many of the rest of us have thought about the connection between our ears and our stomachs.

We recall many other instances when our own children used language creatively in play. One of our favorites occurred during the summer, maybe a decade ago, when we toured the Grand Canyon. One evening we perched on a promontory to take pictures of the incredible rainbow-filled sunset. After a while, our daughters became bored and turned to a fallen tree for entertainment. The trunk became a shuttle bus with Cherie the conductor and Aimee the passenger. "Next stop Exclamation Point," Cherie declared, very much in keeping with her surroundings, for the canyon truly was a sight to exclaim about!

Creativity doesn't limit itself to purely verbal expression. All children are naturally imaginative in some aspect of their lives. Some express their creativity through mechanics, building large and complex structures out of Tinker Toys, erector sets, and the like. Others are artistically endowed. They may paint and sculpt fascinating works of art. Creativity can also mean the ability to use a common object in some new or unusual way. In fact, educational psychologists say that there are over 100 different kinds of intelligence. Each can incorporate its own brand of creativity.

In addition, some children are *convergent* thinkers. They seek to solve problems by bringing ideas together in a logical way. Others are *divergent* thinkers. They are always bringing up new ideas and spinning one from the next. They see connections between ideas that are lost on other children.

Creativity is an important part of your child's kindergarten readiness and her future. A child who allows her imagination to run free will come up with new ideas about how the world works. Such a child may grow one day into the scientist who makes the creative leap in solving the puzzle of the universe or in understanding the workings of the human mind.

INDIVIDUAL ACTIVITIES CAN ENCOURAGE CREATIVITY

We fondly recall the hours our daughter Aimee used to spend constructing a tent city in the backyard. She would haul together two or three patio chairs as the supports for the tent and throw an old beach blanket over these. Then, she would drag over chaise lounge pads for the floor and decorate the exterior with camellia petals she had plucked from the surrounding shrubs. When her friend Ali joined her the city would take on massive proportions, sprawling across half the backyard.

Finally, ensconced in her new home, Aimee would cook up pies made of mud, berries from the privet hedges, and fallen leaves and blades of grass. These she would "serve" to us and to our poor dog, Kasha, who both relished and resisted all the attention being lavished upon her. From time to time, Aimee would even bring her blankie outside and fall asleep in the cozy home she had built for herself in the yard.

No organized class in the world—no gymnastics, swimming, violin, ballet, or crafts—could command Aimee's attention to the degree that this spontaneous endeavor did. She continued to play this game in one form or another for many years.

We bring this up because we feel that we can't stress enough the importance of spontaneous, imaginative play for your preschooler. Sometimes, as parents, we get caught up in the fads and fashions of the day. If we see that Jessica's parents are providing her with piano lessons, tumbling, and computer literacy at four years old, we fear that our own child will miss out on important and enriching experiences. And so we enroll Samantha as well.

But the overscheduled child can also be a stressed child. Kids require off-time to let their imaginations roam free. Their natural, uninhibited fantasy world needs to be encouraged and supported, even if it seems unbridled to you. Believe it or not, boredom also has its positive aspects. It pushes your youngster to create an activity for herself that will take care of her own needs. So, while it's true that structured activities have their place and value, they should not substitute for your preschooler's unstructured playtime.

In some ways, the importance of unstructured time also applies to the toys you purchase. Computer-driven dolls and teddy bears that talk to your child, for example, have a limited life. They are great novelties at first, but once the thrill of the technology wears off, your child is apt to abandon the toy. Its range is too limited. More generic playthings such as building blocks, Tinker Toys, Bristle Blocks, clay or Play-Doh, crayons and water paints, dolls and toy kitchens, dress-up clothes, and puppets hold much more appeal in the long run. Your preschooler projects herself into each of these. Every time she plays with them, she creates a new and wondrous world.

Imaginative play is serious business for your child. When Aimee made her mud pies she acted as if she were really cooking. Indeed, to her, she *was*. We pretended to enjoy the "treats" she offered us because to respond otherwise would have denied her experience. When you encourage your child's spontaneous creativity during play, you participate in a moment of intimacy with her. She has let you into her inner world.

DOES TELEVISION DISCOURAGE THE THREE CS?

Aimee's kindergarten teacher is adamant in her conviction that television serves to limit preschoolers' language skills. We also believe that TV provides an unrealistic image of the world in which complex problems are solved in 30 to 60 minutes, often through the use of deception and manipulation if not violence. These are not values that we wished to teach our children. In addition, even good children's programming like "Sesame Street" teaches lessons in very short bursts of energy. These fleeting segments are great for younger children but they do little to enhance the attention spans of kids readying themselves for kindergarten.

The debate about the positive and/or negative effects of TV on children has raged on probably since our own childhoods. While most of us have come out of the "age of television" more or less intact, there is still a good deal of truth to the idea that children who watch lots of TV may be experiencing some negative vicarious learning. They may pick up attitudes and behaviors such as aggression or sex-role and racial stereotypes from indiscriminate TV watching.

A recent article in the *New York Times* entitled "What Are Commercials Selling to Children?" is highly critical of the content and messages conveyed in those ubiquitous ads. The author, John J. O'Connor, makes the following valid points:

> Certainly, the commercials specifically aimed at young audiences are, at the very least, suspect. They don't only sell products—sugar-saturated and grease-clogged junk food—that arrogantly ignore today's nutritional campaigns. They also sell language ("Ain't life delicious," says the candy spot). More to the point, they sell attitudes and values. Equally as disturbing as the sexism on so many commercials is the racism, even if unintentional. . . .
>
> Consider the parade of blue-eyed dolls—Beach Blast Barbie, Hula-Hoop Maxie, Cool Times Barbie. . . . Just about every commercial makes a point of mentioning the doll's hair, which is invariably blond and silky. "She's got the best hair," brags one commercial. Is there a message here for the black and Hispanic children with dark curled hair?

Whether or not children's programming increases preschoolers' aggressive behavior and sex-role and racial stereotyping, we never looked fondly upon TV in our household. We decided that it was "brain candy" for our kids. It was fun and possibly pleasurable, but most shows other than those offered on public TV stations and the occasional nature program delivered little nourishment or substance. On the other hand, we felt we had to be realistic. To deny our kids any children's programming other than "Sesame Street" would exclude them, in some ways, from the culture at large.

Indeed, if we can carry the analogy to candy a bit further, we would say that a child who is forbidden any sweets whatsoever will go hog-wild once offered the opportunity to eat at will—mostly out of a feeling of deprivation. We didn't want to create TV addicts later in life. So, rather than abolish TV in the house altogether, we sought to limit it. As preschoolers, our kids could watch only a certain times and only certain shows. Often these were educational programs like "Sesame Street" and "Electric Company."

We allowed cartoons no more than one hour a day, and we carefully monitored "adult" comedies. Dramas were verboten. We often used the sitcoms as a resource for conversation. Susan didn't have the stomach to watch the shows through with the kids and often she was busy preparing dinner during their TV hour. But she would pop in every ten minutes or so to see what was happening with the "Brady Bunch" or "Three's Company." If she felt that a show was sexist, violent, or dishonest in its approach, she would make pointed comments about what she felt was objectionable. Ads sometimes drove her wild. Later, she and the kids would talk about the attitudes portrayed so that the children wouldn't absorb them unconsciously.

Of course, every family operates differently and TV serves many different functions in different households. Sometimes it's the only way to keep the kids out from underfoot when you're hungry, tired, and in a hurry to make dinner. And, Lord knows, TV is a great way to keep your tykes occupied when they awaken at 6:30 Saturday morning raring to go.

Probably the best way to create your family policy about TV is to first look at your own TV habits and attitudes. Do you use this form of entertainment to wind down after a hard day at work? Do you just want to "veg out," couch-potato style? If so, you may have a hard time convincing your preschooler that TV isn't all that good for him. After all, you seem to enjoy it! Sometimes compromise is necessary. In the process, it may help to ask yourself the question "How can I use TV to encourage my child's curiosity, conversation, and creativity?"

To that end, you can help your preschooler make the best use of TV by watching with him and discussing the content and attitudes that you find worthy of comment. Ask pointed questions to help pique your child's curiosity and creativity. Engage him in conversation about what he thinks is going to happen next or why a character is acting silly. Television is here to stay, so you might as well use it to your child's advantage.

In the final analysis, a child who engages in curiosity, conversation, and creativity is a *thinking* child whose mind is always alert to new possibilities. That, to us, is the essence of kindergarten readiness.

This first part of *Kindergarten—It Isn't What It Used to Be* has helped you look at some of the more theoretical issues involved in kindergarten readiness. In the next part of this book, we'll get down to the nuts and bolts of school, beginning with an introduction to the mechanics of kindergarten.

PART 2

THE SCHOOL EXPERIENCE

CHAPTER 7

Happy Trails: What You Should Look for in a Good Kindergarten Program

We'd like to begin this chapter with a bit of a disclaimer: It's difficult for parents to evaluate a kindergarten program objectively. As parents, we all have the limitation of being a product of our own environment. Our perceptions are molded by experience. Every child (and every parent who is attached to that child) has different needs. It's important for you to be aware of your own point of view without necessarily projecting it onto your preschooler. Your needs may not be his.

In this chapter, we will supply some markers to help you identify appropriate kindergarten policy and to indicate what you should look for in adequate after-school care. First, let's take a look at what makes evaluation of a kindergarten program a rather difficult task.

THE RELATIVITY OF A "GOOD" KINDERGARTEN

During Aimee's toddlerhood, she participated in a neighborhood play group, where four or five mothers and their children got together once a week for socialization and coffee. Just about all of the mothers of two-year-olds also had preschoolers who were on the verge of starting kindergarten together that fall at our local public school. So, in addition to discussing potty training and refereeing fights, the women also reflected upon the impending momentous step into elementary school that their older children were about to take.

Each mother had certain expectations. Susan, for example, hoped that kindergarten would live up to its billing as an "open structure" school in which the children could advance at their own pace rather than at the tempo set by the majority of the students. Other mothers expressed differing needs.

When the mothers met as a group three weeks after the school year had begun, they all expressed disappointment. Each woman felt that the school was inadequate in some way—all different. It became clear that the school could not be all things to all people. Each mother's conscious or unconscious expectations had colored her view of the kindergarten experience.

That's not unusual. Often as parents we relive our own pasts through our children, using our experiences as yardsticks. Sometimes in our need to correct what we perceive as mistakes of the past, we lose sight of the fact that our children are separate beings from us. They have different parents than we did and life experiences that are all their own. Their needs may be quite distinct from what ours were when we were five years old or from what we imagine them to be today. And that's important to keep in mind if you're evaluating or seeking out a kindergarten for your child.

BEWARE OF "GROUP-THINK"

A further word of caution on choosing a school: Parents sometimes get into a "group-think" situation. All the parents in the neighborhood are sending their kids to the "best" school, so you take it on their say-so that the school will be appropriate for your kids too. Before you make such a big decision, you must ask yourself, "best" in terms of what—reputation, or what is really good for *your* child?

We had such an experience when choosing a preschool for Aimee. Most of our neighbors sent their children to one school in the vicinity. Aimee's best friend, Ali, was enrolling there. When Susan went to observe, however, she knew immediately that the school was not for our child. She found the teachers to be even more controlling than she was—their approach echoed her own parenting style too closely. Susan wanted a nursery school that would compensate for her own tendency to impose too much structure. She felt that Aimee needed an environment in which she could explore more freely and get good and dirty. She sought out a different school at some distance from our home.

The issue appeared again when Aimee was entering high school. She began the ninth grade in one of the most prestigious schools in the city, if not the nation. The school has tremendous resources, equipment, and a glorious list of alumni.

As marvelous as the school might have been, unfortunately, we found that it was not good for our child. Of what value were the cyclotron, planetarium, and television station, the quiet carpeted hallways and air conditioning, when she was walking around feeling inadequate all the time? Aimee's self-confidence was at an all-time low.

After many attempts at rectifying the situation, eventually we came to see that the school was more interested in its reputation than in the welfare of the individual students. With Aimee's grudging assent, we transferred her out of there—much to her immediate sorrow (at missing her many friends) but to her eventual relief at finding a program where she could be appreciated for being herself.

No matter what a school's reputation or stated philosophy, an educational institution is only as good as its teachers and counselors. Every once in a while, unfortunately, you find a bad apple in the bunch. It's important not to take a school's reputation for granted. Evaluate and choose wisely and with vigilance.

THE EIGHT CARDINAL CRITERIA

As we all know, the educational scene isn't what it was when we were children. Whereas, traditionally, kids went to the neighborhood public school that was closest to home, today, according to a recent article in the *New York Times*, "at least a dozen states and scores of local school districts now allow parents to choose which public school their children will attend." This approach, aimed at making the schools compete for students and thus improve the quality of education, is part of President Bush's program to strengthen our schools.

In addition, many affluent and middle-class parents are in a position to send their children to private kindergartens and elementary schools. Even when the local elementary school offers excellent programs, they may opt for the smaller class size and increased attention that a private education can provide. They may also view private schooling as a way to give their children an advantage when it comes to college placement and an eventual career.

If you have your choice of kindergarten—or even if you don't but want to get the best out of your local public school—you need to know what you should look for.

If you have a choice, contact a wide range of schools that you may be interested in. When you call to ask pertinent questions about the programs offered, plan your questions in advance and decide what you'd like to hear. For example, if the continuing development of social skills is important for your child, ask what portion of the day is allotted to fun and playtime. A program that is purely academic may not be appropriate for your five-year-old.

Ask how long the present director has been at the school as well as how long the staff has been together. Some private schools have horrendous turnover problems. Good friends of ours unwittingly sent their daughter to one such unstable institution. Linda had five (count 'em) different teachers during her kindergarten year. This was terribly stressful to her (as it would be to any of us) and caused headaches, stomachaches, and a general distrust of the school environment. Fortunately, our friends were wise enough to pull Linda out before further damage was done. She is now happily ensconced in a public first grade.

The private schools that pay the highest salaries are more successful in keeping their staff. Indeed, these teachers may be more dedicated and committed to the institution. If you have the time, you might do a comparative study of teacher salaries to assess probable turnover.

If you're looking into private schools, ask about the qualifications of the principal and staff. The director or principal should hold a master's degree or its equivalent (such as supervised training) in education or educational psychology.

Teachers need not be certified by the state to teach in some private schools. You'll want to know how experienced the unlicensed teachers are. At least one year of experience should be a minimum. (In California, for example, a teacher is required to have one year of student teaching before qualifying for a teaching credential. Unlicensed teachers have no such requirement.) Five years of experience is better. Ask whether the kindergarten teacher has specific training in early-childhood education and whether she has attended recent continuing-education seminars or other in-service training.

If the answers are satisfactory, schedule a visit. Be sure to use your intuition. You'll know when a principal sounds enthusiastic and positive. Moreover, use the questions you ask to discover the principal's attitude toward parents. His or her patience with your concerns is a good barometer for patience with your children.

Plan to spend an hour observing the classroom. Believe us, after one hour you'll know whether the school is right. Did you walk away calm and relaxed or agitated and relieved to be out of there? Each school has a "feel" or an attitude that communicates itself non-verbally, so trust your instincts.

Ideally, the school should feel nurturing and warm. If you have any doubts whatsoever, don't commit yourself. Continue your investigations. Just because a school has a waiting list doesn't mean it's the best for your child. It may just be popular, mediocre, and convenient. The following are some specific points to watch for during your visit.

How Does the Teacher Handle Conflicts?

The teacher or principal should discipline disruptive five-year-olds using a "time-out" system. The limits or expectations for behavior should be quite clear. If a child oversteps the limits, the adult in charge should calmly explain to him that his behavior is unacceptable and that he will have to take a time-out for five minutes in order to think about what he has done. The erring youngster is removed from the ongoing activity and seated in a boring spot for the duration. After the requisite time, he should be reintegrated into the classroom activity without further recrimination.

Rarely if ever should the teacher be wagging a finger, blaming, threatening, or shouting. In addition, the teacher should talk to the child by bending down or kneeling, rather than standing over him, as we explained in Chapter 6.

Also observe how the teacher handles conflicts between and among children. The socialization skills begun in preschool continue to be refined in kindergarten and beyond. You'll want a teacher who is deeply aware of how difficult it is for children to grasp these concepts and is capable of helping youngsters settle their own disputes peaceably.

Is the Day Structured or Unstructured?

Notice whether the whole class is engaged in activities as a unit or whether children are allowed to move freely from one activity area to another as their interests or needs dictate. The classroom routine may use a combination of these two teaching styles. Neither is inherently right or wrong. You'll have to assess your own preference.

In your observations, notice whether some children are left by themselves without direction. It's important that all youngsters be included in activities, especially the child who tends to withdraw. If the school is sensitive to this type of child, then it is sure to take into account all children.

Is There an Imagination Corner?

Five-year-olds still need to play. Make sure that the kindergarten has at least one corner in which the children can go to dress up, play house, and play with blocks and trucks. Imaginative play is an important part of child development at this age and should not be shunted aside prematurely in favor of pure academics.

Is There a Science Corner?

Children learn many important lessons (about life and death, about responsibility, about the food chain and the cycles of nature) from the care of living plants and animals. Every kindergarten classroom should have some sort of natural science corner that includes small animals like bunnies, gerbils, or guinea pigs and plants grown from seed.

How Do the Teachers and Principal Communicate with Parents?

Are there letters, report cards, face-to-face conferences, phone calls? How would you communicate your concerns to the teacher? How open is she to your input?

What's the Teacher-Student Ratio?

States mandate classroom size for public schools. Kindergarten classes are usually smaller than second or third grade so that children can get more individualized attention. Private schools may have the funding to provide a much smaller teacher-student ratio than you would find in a public school. This may be great but, if you recall our discussion in Chapter 4, it may not necessarily be to your child's benefit. Your youngster may need a pool of many children from whom to choose friends.

All things being equal, we'd recommend a more qualified teacher who is warm and nurturing toward her twenty charges over a stern or withdrawn teacher in a classroom of only eight kids.

Do the Children Seem Happy?

This is probably the most important criterion. Are the kindergarteners smiling and laughing or do they appear glum and bored? Is the classroom chaotic or do you observe the quiet hum of young excited minds at work? One way we assessed our children's happiness quotient was to note whether they brought home songs and stories from school.

What about Life beyond Kindergarten?

Constancy and stability are important for your child. Unless there are grave and serious problems, once she enrolls in a particular school system you may be loathe to transfer her to another setting. In addition, she may be reluctant to give up the security of familiar places and faces. When you're evaluating a kindergarten classroom, you may be committing yourself to an entire six-year elementary school program. In truth, it would be misleading to divorce the kindergarten class from the rest of the school. Take the time to explore the school program beyond kindergarten. It will come upon you sooner than you think.

WHAT IF YOU DON'T HAVE A CHOICE?

Come September, the vast majority of children will attend their local public schools, as our kids did. The pointers that we list above, however, can come in handy even if you don't have a choice. You can keep them in mind when you go for your kindergarten visit with your child (see Chapter 8). It's important that you form an opinion about the school, for even if you don't have a choice as to which school your child attends, you may have some influence on the course of his education once he gets there.

Try to view the elementary school as an extension of yourself and your community. If it's public and supported by city and state tax funds, then in essence you along with your neighbors own the school. Even in a private school, your tuition is essential for funding programs. You can actively lobby for the school to reflect your values. Barring that, you can organize and take your case to the school board. Your point of view is important.

WHEN THERE ARE PROBLEMS

If you're not happy with a school-related situation, then by all means speak up! We had this experience during our older daughter's first days at elementary school. Cherie was quite precocious and Susan was in the habit of pushing her ahead. We had almost decided to have her skip kindergarten altogether, but the fact that our local school offered a K-1-2 class along with the regular kindergarten helped change our minds.

Susan thought that the combination kindergarten, first- and second-grade class was ideal since our daughter would be able to read at a higher level. In theory it could have worked because Cherie was one of the oldest children in her class. But, as we all know, theory and reality don't always match.

The first day of school, Cherie was called up to the front of the auditorium and placed in the combination class. Susan was thrilled. She was sure that our daughter would get the benefit of this innovative class set-up.

Everything changed, however, when Susan met Cherie at the classroom door that afternoon. Cherie had not had a good day. The teacher, Ms. K., was mean and cold. There was no talking, no time to play. She made the children line up in straight rows of boys and girls ranked by size from shortest to tallest (we thought that old-fashioned practice had gone the way of the Edsel and the Hula-Hoop).

What was worse, Cherie and a classmate, a friend from our street, had held hands—as if they were hanging on for dear life—frightened by the unpleasant specter of elementary school life. Ms. K. yelled at them to drop their hands when she arranged them in line. The children were practically in tears.

When Susan and the mother of this little boy caught sight of the terrified look in their children's eyes, they didn't waste a minute. They marched straight to the principal's office and demanded that their children be put back into the straight kindergarten class with the rest of their peers. So much for pushing Cherie ahead. After several days, the changes were effectuated, and both families felt great relief.

There was an important lesson in this episode for us—and therefore for you: You can make a difference in your child's education (even when you can't choose the school) by your attention and involvement. Listen to your children's assertions, take them seriously, and prepare a course of action. Children rarely complain for no reason.

GET THE MOST OUT OF YOUR SCHOOL—GET INVOLVED

When you are evaluating the kindergarten program, make sure to ask how you can get involved. Every school has some sort of parent organization. You may want to become active in the PTA or the School Site Council. If you work during the day and can't attend daytime meetings, lobby for alternate meeting times. You can volunteer to flip pancakes for the Sunday Pancake Breakfast fund-raiser or to sell popcorn and paint faces at the weekend Spring Fair.

If you have a skill that is useful in an elementary curriculum and can spare the time, you may want to become an occasional classroom volunteer. For example, it's great fun to give a simple cooking lesson to a kindergarten class. You might spend 30 minutes one morning talking to the children about your job or career. The teacher could build a series of lessons around your visit.

You can even help the kids in the sixth grade apply their stage makeup or volunteer to run the videotape during the evening performance. Activities with the older grades make you part of the greater school community, and they help you and your child get to know the "big" kids. Such shared involvement will render the older children less threatening and can put you in touch with the school's long-term needs, which may eventually impact you.

To rephrase President Kennedy's famous statement, we would urge you to ask not what your school can do for your children but ask, rather, what you can do for your school. The benefits of your involvement are numerous. First of all, the institution itself and all of the children in it will be enriched by your efforts—be it your input on how to enhance the gifted children's program or your argument that additional crossing guards are needed. Second, you will be enriched by a sense of accomplishment and a feeling of community that comes from working with others toward a common goal. Involvement is a great way to meet new people. Finally, it just makes good sense because it's good for your kids.

Our daughters always felt proud of our involvement. For them it meant that we took their schooling seriously and, therefore, they took it seriously. They were always excited when we visited school. They could see that their school was a priority for us—and that's an important message to give.

In addition, it's a mistake to think that once you send your five-year-old off to kindergarten, your job is done. (We can tell you from our current experience that parenting doesn't end at the college level, either!) The teacher can't take care of everything. She may be pulled in forty directions at once. Your involvement and inquiries about particular issues and problems may help to focus her attention on your child's needs. Your relationship may be purely by note or phone conversation, but at least you will feel that you have made needed contact.

We have to admit that we also had ulterior motives in becoming active parents. We learned, rather early on, that the parents who were involved, who contributed to the school's well-being, seemed to have an inside track to the principal's office. The squeaky wheel definitely got the oil. It's not that the principal played favorites. It's just that when there was a problem—say, in a child's class placement—he was apt to rectify the situation more quickly when he knew the parents.

Involved parents also seemed to know which teachers had the most to offer in each grade, and they saw to it that their children were placed in those classes. Unfortunately, the youngsters whose parents could not or would not get involved sometimes got the short end of the stick. If all parents were to become involved, they would provide the much-needed impetus for positive change. After all, we all want the best the school has to offer, and we all want the best for our children.

A WORD ABOUT AFTER-SCHOOL CARE

Most kindergartens still offer half-day sessions, even though, according to the U.S. Bureau of Labor Statistics, 71 percent of all married mothers with school-age children are employed. The majority of children entering kindergarten these days, therefore, need supervision for the rest of the day. You may be obliged to seek alternative care for the afternoon hours, especially if your preschooler has been enrolled in a full-day program at a nursery school or day-care center. The same guidelines that you use in evaluating kindergarten can be of help in seeking out an appropriate after-school program.

Depending on the community, there are many possibilities for after-school care. The YMCA, religious institutions, public parks, private after-school "camps," parent cooperatives, and community centers may offer the services you need. Many provide bus transportation directly from school.

Check out each of these facilities as carefully as you would the school. After all, your youngster may spend as many hours at the after-school program as she does in kindergarten. It's also wise to line up the right program and visit it with your child long before she has to enroll. (Some programs are inactive during the summer or convert to summer day camps run by different administrators.) There will be many adjustments to make those first few weeks of September, and you don't want to be in a funk about adequate day care along with starting school. It's wise to take care of this early.

What should you look for in an after-school program? That depends on the kind of programs available in your area and your price range. Here are some general questions to ask yourself and the staff in making your assessment.

★ Is there a feeling of order and calm, even if the children become dirty from play?

★ Is imaginative play encouraged?

★ Is there adequate equipment for climbing and other gross motor activities?

★ Can the kids let off steam after being cooped up in school for several hours or must they conform to strict rules?

★ How does the staff handle discipline and conflicts?

★ Do the children have a place to put their belongings?

★ Are the kindergarteners given lunch and afternoon snack?

★ Is there a nap time or a quiet place for the children who need it?

★ What are the director's and the staff's qualifications?

★ What is the counselor/ or teacher/child ratio?

★ Are the bathroom facilities adequate and clean and are children encouraged to wash their hands after using the facilities?

★ Are the bus drivers licensed to drive buses? What is their safety record?

★ What is the policy if a child becomes hurt or sick while under the care of the facility?

★ Is this a glorified baby-sitting service or will your child be stimulated and challenged by the program?

★ Can you contact references, other parents whose youngsters are enrolled in the program?

★ Do the children seem happy?

Now that you have a sense of what you should expect from the school environment, it's time to introduce your preschooler to the mechanics of kindergarten during a visit to school. Keep our recommendations in mind as you take your child through the steps outlined in the next chapter.

CHAPTER 8

The School Visit: Introducing Your Preschooler to the Mechanics of Kindergarten

In gathering our research for *Kindergarten—It Isn't What It Used to Be*, we came across a children's book that we thought was apropos. *Annabelle Swift, Kindergartener* by Amy Schwartz is about a five-year-old whose older sister decides to prepare her for the big day. "I'm going to teach you the fancy stuff, Annabelle," Lucy says. "Tomorrow they'll know you're *my* sister."

Lucy proceeds to instruct Annabelle in a most unorthodox manner about what to expect at kindergarten. For example, she uses their mother's makeup to review colors. Lipstick is not really red but "Raving Scarlet." She describes the color of eyeshadow she smears on her eyelids as "Blue Desire."

As you can imagine, this wreaks havoc with Annabelle's first day at school. When the class goes into the "concept corner" to identify colored lollipops, Annabelle jumps to her feet and shouts, "Blue Desire!" at the sight of light blue construction paper. Eventually she saves the day by being the only child in the class able to count all the nickels and pennies for milk money. As a reward, she is allowed to walk to the cafeteria to pick up the class's midmorning snack.

This story, while certainly amusing to your five-year-old, also carries several valuable lessons. One of them is that faulty preparation or overpreparation can be worse than none at all. Annabelle already knew how to count to 100 using money before Lucy's tutoring. In fact, Lucy's suggestions for Annabelle's success in math are hilarious. "Remember," she says, "to ask plenty of questions, Anna-belle. Teachers like that. Are there any numbers less than zero? And what's the number after infinity, anyway?" Annabelle decides not to ask about zero or infinity during the arithmetic lesson. Smart girl.

On the other hand, Lucy's heart probably is in the right place even if her methods are a bit wacky. Your preschooler should be introduced to kindergarten in some fashion before the big day. Familiarity with the classroom procedures and routines helps to dissipate her fear of the unknown. She can keep images in her mind of what school will be like. These will ease her passage through this transition and may help to allay some of her separation anxiety.

The best way to introduce the mechanics of kindergarten to your child is by paying the school a visit in the spring before your pre-schooler is slated to begin. Sometimes, when a large proportion of a preschool class is matriculating to the same school, both schools arrange a group orientation visit for children and/or parents. If this is not the case, call ahead to inquire about the best time for your personal tour. You may need to arrange your observation directly with the teacher since certain days may be inopportune for guests. Ask if you can spend the whole morning (or afternoon). This may mean your taking a day off from work, but it's well worth it. The kindergarten visit is that important.

GETTING THE HANG OF KINDERGARTEN ROUTINES

The following is a commonsense discussion of the routines that your preschooler may witness during his visit. You may want to answer his questions during your observation, when they're still fresh. While he's busy absorbing the sights and sounds of kindergarten life, you might mentally assess the classroom concerning the issues we discussed in the previous chapter.

The Trip to School

It is important to get off on the right foot—perhaps literally. Long before school starts, your preschooler should become familiar with how he is going to get to kindergarten. If the school is only a few blocks away, you'll probably want him to walk. In that case, walk the route with him several times during the summer. You may want to indicate familiar landmarks along the way. If there are traffic lights to obey, make sure your child understands how to respond.

We lived close to our elementary school but the children had to cross two very busy city streets to get there. For safety's sake, we did not feel comfortable letting them walk to or from school alone until they were in the second grade and somewhat more responsible. We made sure they knew they had to hold a parent's or baby-sitter's hand during street crossing—no racing ahead. We also drummed into their little curly heads that they should never accept candy or rides from strangers or talk to strangers who pull up next to them in their cars.

If you will be driving your child to school, your task is fairly simple. Take a few trial trips so that your preschooler becomes familiar with the route. If he will be taking a school bus, you should start your preparation in advance of the summer. You may want to follow the bus one morning (if you can stand the fumes) from your stop to the other ones along the way until you reach school.

Once school starts, your youngster might feel safer if he and a friend board the bus at the same stop or if they look for each other en route so that they can sit together. In that way, he won't feel so alone on the big, noisy vehicle. See what you can arrange in advance. If he finds the bus itself intimidating, you might want to make several practice trips on municipal transportation, just for the feel and the fun of it. Don't forget to stress bus safety rules like staying in one's seat and not shouting.

For the first few months at least, if not the whole year, wait with your child at the bus stop until his ride arrives. Your presence, goodbye kiss, and wave will be reassuring to him.

Lining Up

In our daughter's school, the arriving kindergarteners were escorted to a special enclosed yard that was separated from the rest of the school. There they had a chance to socialize until the bell rang signaling the start of the day. At that point, after greeting her pupils, the teacher asked the children to settle down and form a line so that they could enter the classroom in an orderly fashion.

Schools operate with some variations. Yours may not require the children to line up before class begins, but you may find other instances in which the teacher demands a certain order. Your rambunctious preschooler may find that kind of structure unfamiliar. She may quail at having to take orders from another adult. Explain to her that the school has certain rules that all of the children obey for the safety and comfort of others. Point out how well the kids listen to their teacher.

Classroom Details

As the kindergarteners take off their coats and settle down, you can spend a moment examining the classroom with your child. The ideal environment is stimulating and reflects the children's point of view. After all, this is their room.

Observe whether the children use individual desks or large tables that can be arranged for group activities. The latter may indicate that the kindergarten stresses socialization as well as academics. Also look for the students' artwork adorning the walls. Our daughters' teachers posted graphs showing each child's progress as a way to give positive reinforcement. Aimee's kindergarten teacher exhibited what she called a "Snaggletooth Puss" chart, showing which of the kindergarteners had lost a front tooth during the year. All of these displays serve to enhance the students' feelings of self-esteem.

Roll Call

Most likely, taking attendance will be an unfamiliar process to your preschooler. Alert him to how the children are all seated quietly on the rug, waiting for their names to be called. The wait may take some patience for your child if there are twenty children in the classroom.

Pledge of Allegiance

The pledge may be the first piece of prose that your child ever memorizes. We all have fond recollections of garbling those words that we hardly understood yet—running them together with such speed that they were indistinguishable one from the other. Your preschooler may be surprised to see the class rise in unison, put their right hands over their hearts, and begin to recite. The class may also sing the national anthem or hymn. There's no reason not to practice these with your preschooler at home, if he's eager to do so. But make it fun, not pressure or work.

Work Time

Your youngster may notice that group and individual learning activities occupy the majority of the school day in kindergarten. This may be quite different from his preschool experience, especially if he has been in a developmental setting that stresses socialization and not academics or if he has spent his days with a baby-sitter. Remember that your visit occurs toward the end of the school year, when the children have matured considerably since the previous September. The level of work activity will probably be more intense than what your youngster will experience when he first begins kindergarten. Reassure him that he will grow into the work load as the year progresses.

Learning Activities and Learning Centers

If your preschooler has been in a rather structured nursery school environment, she may feel confused by a kindergarten that embraces an open structure model in which children move from one activity to another at their own pace. Learning centers set up around the room offer a wide variety of activities from which to choose, from exercises in writing the alphabet to art projects. Help her see that when children finish one activity, they move on to another.

Bathroom Rules

Bathrooms at school are quite different from those at home. If your child has been in a preschool that had many toilets in a row, he will be used to the idea of children going to the bathroom at the same time. In addition, he may also be familiar with the louder and more vigorous flush, the less-than-cushy toilet paper, the use of the soap dispenser, and paper towels. If he has been in a day-care home or with a baby-sitter, these facilities may be new to him. Some little boys, for example, may never have had the opportunity to use a urinal. In that case, make sure to visit public toilets when you're out at a ball game or department store to help him gain some familiarity.

Schools and teachers may set their own rules about when kindergarteners can use the bathroom. In some instances, the toilets are in a small room off the classroom and children can run in to use them whenever the need arises. In other situations, the toilets may be down the hall and the kindergartners may need to be escorted or take a hall pass.

In either case, your preschooler needs to know that he can ask to use the bathroom. Margery Kranyik, author of *Starting School*, points out that children may need to be encouraged to ask permission. "Because children are often afraid to ask permission," she explains, "they spend their school day in total discomfort. The minute they arrive home after school, they make a dash for the bathroom." Also, to save them embarrassment, make sure they don't use family pet names for toilet functions.

Recess

At preschool, the whole day seems like recess. In kindergarten, your child will note definite demarcations between work time and play time. Pay attention to where the children spend their break. Do they go out on the playground or do they have their milk and cookies in the classroom? Does the teacher collect milk money? Do the children use the bathroom? Ask if the routine changes during inclement weather.

If your child suffers from food allergies or if you don't want her to participate in milk and cookies, ask the teacher (at an appropriate moment) about alternative snack arrangements such as sugar-free cookies, carrot sticks, or apples. You should make plans for alternatives well in advance so that your child won't have to deal with any confusion about snacks on the first days of school.

You'll probably find that many other parents have similar concerns. If the teacher is really astute, at some point in the school year she may use a classroom discussion about fresh fruits and vegetables as a way to teach about good nutrition.

Quiet Time

Following recess, there may be a period of time in which the children participate in a quiet group activity. The teacher may read a story or work with a felt board and numbers. Point out to your child whether certain standards of behavior are expected at these times. Must the youngsters remain quietly in their seats during the lesson?

Outdoor Activities

Most likely, the kindergarten will be equipped with some kind of climbing apparatus or jungle gym, as well as other paraphernalia that promote gross motor development along with socialization. Our daughters' kindergarten yard sported discarded tires, for example, that made marvelous toys for climbing, rolling, bouncing—and sharing. The children could also practice throwing and catching balls, building houses out of giant hollow blocks, jumping rope, digging in the sandbox, and creating art projects using messy materials.

Show your child what's available and ask the kindergarten teacher whether your child can try out some of the equipment. Depending on the school's insurance considerations, this may or may not be allowed.

The "Big" Kids

Some kindergartens are entirely self-contained, while in others the children mix with other grades. Your preschooler may be intimidated by the sheer size and heft of the older kids. If the kindergarten class does integrate with the rest of the school, have him pay attention to how the interactions occur.

In some schools, peer tutors—children a year or two older—come into the room to assist the kindergarten teacher in teaching reading. In that case, the younger children make friends with the "old-timers," who lose their aura of threat. If your child is afraid of bullies, show him that there are lots of teachers in the schoolyard to whom he should go if he feels threatened—he does not have to deal with bullies all by himself. Reassure your preschooler that, in time, he will feel comfortable around the big kids and one day he'll be a "big kid" himself.

Lunchtime

Some kindergartens are all-day programs. In that case, you'll want to follow the class to the cafeteria or yard for lunch. Note whether the youngsters are taken to the bathroom before lunch to wash their hands. Show your preschooler how the children line up to buy their lunches. You might even buy one to sample the fare. Other kids bring food from home but buy drinks at school. See how that is accomplished, and note how much money your child will need to bring to school. (Usually, the principal sends home this information in a parent bulletin before the first day.) Point out where the children eat and what they do with their trash (hopefully, they throw it into the trash can!) once they've finished.

After lunch, children usually have time to play. Do they use balls, jump ropes, and jungle gyms? Again, pay attention to whether or not the older children are mixed in with the kindergarteners. If so, refer back to our suggestions on dealing with older children.

End-of-the-Day Routine

Just as the start of the day has its order, so does the close. The kindergarteners may have to dress themselves in heavy coats and boots to prepare for stormy weather. Parents may pick their children up at the outer gate or at the classroom door. The teacher makes sure that the youngsters using bus transportation for after-school care or home have boarded the correct vehicle. In most cases, the teacher does not leave until all of the children have been safely sent on their way. Point out these various routines to your preschooler.

A DAY OF IMPRESSIONS: LET'S TALK ABOUT IT

On your way home, you and your preschooler have a marvelous opportunity to reflect on what you have just experienced. Ask her what she thinks about the class, the students, and the teacher. Be enthusiastic and positive about all of the wonderful things she's going to learn at school. You want kindergarten to be an experience she looks forward to, not one she dreads.

While you're at it, you may bring up the various socioeconomic and ethnic groups represented in the classroom. Kindergarten may be the first time that your child encounters the variety of cultures represented in our country. Indeed, in the melting pot that now characterizes Los Angeles, our daughters spent their elementary school years with children of all racial and ethnic backgrounds, including youngsters from Russia, Japan, Vietnam, Korea, Israel, England, Germany, Guatemala, Mexico, and Iran. This multiethnicity enriched their educational experience. Kindergarten is an important time for children to learn that people are people the world over.

REALISTIC EXPECTATIONS

Another important point to bear in mind is that it takes a good deal of time for your child—or anyone, for that matter—to feel absolutely comfortable in a new situation. Nursery school director Jane Zuckerman pointed out to us in a conversation that adults usually need two to three months in a new job before they lose that scared feeling in the pit of their stomach. It's unrealistic to expect your preschooler to adjust to kindergarten after a single visit, or even after two weeks. In Chapter 10 we will cover adjustments to the stress of separation more fully, but keep it in mind during your visit.

Your day together at kindergarten will serve to prepare your preschooler for what's to come, but it will take several months before he's completely at home in his new environment. Undue pressure on him to adjust quickly may only make matters worse. Take it easy. This is a time to enjoy.

As you reflect on all you've seen and heard, give some thought to how you perceived the kindergarten teacher. While no instructor is perfect, in the next chapter we offer some ideas about how the "ideal" kindergarten teacher should act with her young charges.

CHAPTER 9

The Loving Gardener:
What to Look for in a
Great Kindergarten Teacher

There is an ancient Zen story that relates significantly to the giant step into kindergarten your youngster is about to take. The tale revolves around an argument among three teachers who debate the proper educational approach.

The first teacher views his pupils as if they were empty vessels into which he must pour information. "They know nothing," he asserts. "I must fill their heads with knowledge."

The second sees his charges as clay for which he is the potter. "I mold and sculpt them," he says, "to conform to the image that I hold as correct."

The third, however, is different. He treats his students as if they were plants and he the gardener. He realizes that each flower, tree, and shrub needs the proper but unique balance of light, water, and nutrients. "I do not water a cactus as I would a rose," he explains, "nor do I nurture a seedling as I would a mature tree."

This latter portrait of a teacher is very apt. Great kindergarten teachers are like loving gardeners. In fact, our term *kindergarten* comes from the German word meaning *children's garden*. It's a place to "grow" children, and the teacher is the person who does the careful nurturing.

THE AWESOME RESPONSIBILITY

When you understand the scope of the task, you can appreciate what a difficult and awesome responsibility it is to be a kindergarten teacher. Your child's future may be in her hands. Interestingly, however, it's not so much the actual curriculum or information the teacher imparts that is crucial. Rather, it's the spirit with which the teacher approaches the teaching and learning situation that can make a significant difference in your youngster's later adjustment to school.

Kindergarten is the time when your five-year-old begins to form all-important attitudes about school, learning, work habits, homework, and his own feelings of competence. As developmental psychologist and educator Dr. David Elkind explains in his book *Miseducation: Preschoolers at Risk*, "Getting to school on time, paying attention, doing a good, neat job promptly are part of the sense of industry acquired at this time. On the other hand, if children experience excessive failure in efforts to meet the demands of schooling, their sense of inferiority, of being less able than others, will be enhanced." During this pivotal year, your child is learning how to learn.

The kindergarten teacher, by her use of positive reinforcement, by her awareness of individual differences among children, and by her application of an integrated approach that takes into account the whole child, helps to sow the seeds from which positive attitudes eventually will blossom. Good feelings about school and a love of learning cultivated during kindergarten may persist for a lifetime.

PROFILE OF THE GREAT KINDERGARTEN TEACHER

What should you expect from a great kindergarten teacher? After reflecting upon our own experiences as parents and after talking with early-childhood educators, child developmentalists, and kindergarten teachers themselves, we have come up with the following list of characteristics that we feel are important. Obviously, no one teacher can embody all of these qualities; this is a wish list, but it's a good place to start. We begin with personal qualities, then classroom aspects and an understanding of how five-year-olds learn. Look for these attributes during your pre-kindergarten classroom visit and in interaction with the teacher once the school year begins.

Before you jump into our compendium of positive attributes, we would like to remind you that your child's success in kindergarten also depends on the relationship established between home and school. That means that you as a parent have important responsibilities, as does your youngster. We will cover your part of the equation in more detail toward the end of this chapter.

She Is Warm

This is a universal must. Your child's kindergarten teacher must love being around young children. A great kindergarten classroom is like a mutual admiration society. Kids bask in their teacher's affection. They can sense her loving attitude in only a few minutes, and they respond in kind.

The kindergarten teacher must know how to express that love by using appropriate voice and touch, even when she is upset. (No shouting, please. It only serves to frighten and intimidate youngsters.) She should be a nurturing individual who knows how to create a caring classroom environment in which her young charges learn to value and respect themselves and each other as individuals.

One expression of the teacher's warmth is her use of positive reinforcement and praise to help motivate her students. You must remember from your own classroom experience that a kind word and a pat on the back were wonderful ways to get you to perform. The child of the 1990s is no different. Praise is a marvelous tool. A simple statement like, "I love the way you're involved in your project, Samantha," can foster positive attitudes about schoolwork.

Even if the youngster has not mastered a task fully, the ideal kindergarten teacher will praise the attempts and baby-steps taken toward the eventual goal. Conversely, criticism and negative statements only serve to undermine self-esteem and creativity. They are very damaging.

If you recall from our discussion in Chapter 7, our daughter's first-day-of-kindergarten experience with a teacher who was cold and demanding and who yelled at the children set every one of our warning bells ringing. Susan felt it was imperative to get Cherie into a more loving environment.

She Is Trustworthy

Susan remembers a time when she mistakenly sidled up to her kindergarten teacher and called her "Mommy." She was very embarrassed when she realized what she had done. Later, when she became a mother herself, she found that such slips of the tongue are rather common among children who love their teachers. Five-year-olds form strong, trusting attachments to their kindergarten teacher. They go to her when they have a problem. They know she will listen and be fair in helping them resolve a conflict. They can share their feelings with her.

An astute teacher will also know what to look for in terms of child abuse and neglect. She will notice if a child is continually unkempt or hungry or comes to school with many bruises and injuries. She will also look for unhealthy aggressiveness in playing with toys and other children or for unusual withdrawal—the more subtle signs of abuse. The teacher's awareness of these issues will help protect the safety of your child as well. Troubled children will be identified and treated, so they will be less likely to engage in overly aggressive play that could hurt classmates.

When children come home from school relaxed and happy and perhaps just a little bit tired, you can rest assured that the teacher has the ability to create a safe environment in the classroom.

She Is Open

Every child has unique needs. Ann, the seventh of eight children, will come to kindergarten with a different set of expectations and requirements than Robert, an only child who has been the apple of his parents' eye. A great kindergarten teacher is open to appreciating these variations. She develops an intuitive awareness of what each student in her class needs in terms of intellectual, physical, and social growth. She is accepting and nonjudgmental about cultural and socioeconomic differences.

Openness also means that the teacher is willing to take her cues from the class's interests. One teacher we spoke to said, "I learn from my kids. I expect them to give me a challenge. Teaching is a reciprocal activity."

Our daughter Aimee's kindergarten teacher, Arla Capps, explained, "Any teacher can sit back year after year and teach the same skills. But if there is no dialogue going on, there may be little real learning. A lot of kids are wonderful rote learners. They memorize the states and capitals, for example, but they never learn how to think for themselves. They just follow adult directions."

The ideal kindergarten teacher is a good listener. Paying attention to her students' many questions and interests helps her determine what to teach.

She Is Flexible

As the loving gardener, the model kindergarten teacher individualizes. She works with what is given, not with her conception of what the child should be or how he should act. She doesn't make the child fit into the curriculum but rather tailors the curriculum to suit the child.

If Melissa is ready and eager to learn how to read, the kindergarten teacher is astute enough to notice and to give the youngster reading instruction. If Paul has no interest in reading yet, she does not push him in that area. If Erica is great at reading but has a lot of trouble obtaining and sharing toys, the teacher focuses on that task with her.

Flexibility also means taking the ball and running with it if the situation arises. If a child brought a bee into class for "Show and Tell," for example, teacher Arla Capps would scrap the lesson she had prepared in favor of the class's excitement and curiosity about insects. A single bee might engender a half-hour give-and-take discussion about insects and their habitat, folowed by an art project relating to the bee. This is what is known as taking advantage of a *teachable moment*. According to Arla, "a rigid teacher cuts off curiosity and learning by religiously sticking to an agenda."

She Encourages Curiosity

The ideal kindergarten teacher stimulates her students to ask questions. In fact, she loves questions. She doesn't just give her students the answers, either. She helps her charges discover their own answers and express themselves in the process.

For example, a kindergarten teacher may bring a stethoscope into class and have the children listen to one another's hearts. She then poses questions that bring forth the students' own queries. She makes discovery an exciting part of learning. Discovery motivates her students to seek out new information. The kindergarteners' natural curiosity and their need to understand their complex world inspire them to become even more involved in learning.

She Provides Resources

Once the children are stimulated, a great kindergarten teacher will show them how to find the information they want. She explains about research skills. She can show the children books, for example, on the circulatory system and read to them about what they have just experienced in listening to heartbeats. They learn from this that they can access many sources of information beyond the spoken word. They also learn that books and reading don't exist in isolation but serve an important purpose: they communicate information. This helps to motivate the children to want to learn to read.

She Has Broad Interests

The more knowledge a kindergarten teacher has, the more interesting her classroom. If the class is dull for the teacher it will also be dull for the children. Unfortunately, five-year-olds are very accepting and don't always recognize how limited their environment might be. The ideal teacher will provide a wide variety of stimulating activities and materials in the classroom, including blocks, games, and safe scientific equipment—not just workbooks, papers, and pencils. She will also be constantly engaged in the process of broadening her own interests so that she can share her newly acquired knowledge with her charges.

She Implements a Curriculum
That Supports Individual Differences

This is a further extension of the quality of flexibility. Some teachers give lip service to individualizing but they don't carry through in practice. It takes a lot of work to assess and develop learning approaches that are appropriate for each child in the class. Yet it's most important that the teacher allow each child to move at his or her own pace. In order to do that, the ideal kindergarten teacher sets up learning centers.

A learning center is an area in the classroom set aside for a specific task. A reading center, for example, may offer two or three tasks arranged by level of difficulty. These accommodate the students' differing developmental levels and show that the teacher understands that concepts can be broken down into their component parts. In an open classroom, students move from center to center during part of the class time.

The center approach allows children to see where they are headed even if they haven't quite grasped the whole concept. For example, at a reading-readiness skills center, Susie and Marci may find letters to manipulate in a puzzle as well as instruction on how to write and sound out the alphabet. Susie can skip to the writing exercise because she is ready for that. Marci needs to play with the puzzle pieces first to gain familiarity with the alphabet. All the while, Marci recognizes that once she has gotten the puzzle right, she can go on to the next step. The two friends discuss their progress. As the class moves forward in its acquisition of skills, the teacher deletes some activities while adding new ones.

The same can be said for math skills, where the teacher can set up objects of different sizes and weights for learning about "bigger" and "smaller," or coins to learn about money, or chips and numerals to learn about the correspondence between objects and numbers. The important idea is that each step in the sequence leads to the next.

In contrast, inappropriate teaching would require all children to learn the same material at the same pace and at the same time. The children would be evaluated against a standardized test score. The teacher would direct all of the activities, using workbooks, lots of stay-in-your-seat-and-keep-quiet time, and strictly controlled lessons. In such a situation, there would be little room for each child's individual needs or inner motivation to learn. All of the direction would come from the teacher.

She Develops an Integrated Curriculum

Young children don't learn by studying individual subject areas or by drills. That approach encourages memorization but doesn't really give the child a sense of the whole. The National Association for the Education of Young Children, the largest organization devoted to early-childhood education in the country, has issued a position paper on good teaching practices for four- and five-year-olds.

> It is possible to drill children until they recite pieces of information such as the alphabet or the numerals from 1 to 20. However, children's responses to rote tasks do not reflect real understanding of the information. For children to understand fully and remember what they have learned . . . the information must be meaningful to the child in context of the child's experience and development.
>
> Learning information in a meaningful context is not only essential for children's understanding and development of concepts, but is also important for stimulating motivation in children. If learning is relevant for children, they are more likely to persist with a task and be motivated to learn.

Jeremy, for example, can't understand that $2 + 3 = 5$ when he attempts the problem on a worksheet, but if he is given two stacks of minicars, one containing two toys and the other three, he is likely to come up with the correct answer.

The ideal kindergarten teacher understands this. She therefore does not isolate activities into separate subjects. For example, she would not say, "Every morning at 9 we do reading and at 10 we do math," and then sit the kids down for paper-and-pencil work and drills. Instead she creates projects for the class, often suggested by their own questions and interests. These projects combine many aspects of the curriculum at once while they permit the children to work with and learn from each other. The great kindergarten teacher acts as a resource person and a guide. She helps her students help their classmates.

A social-studies project such as creating and running a "grocery store" involves skills on many levels. The children make plans about setting up the store. They write (using their own spelling) or dictate their ideas to the teacher. They may read or have stories read to them about stores. They may paint representations of stores in the neighborhood, or they may use cardboard to construct their own "market." They use numbers to deal with the prices of objects in the store. They must learn the values of coins, and they begin to understand about addition and subtraction. ("If I have five apples and you buy one, how many do I have left?") All the while, the kindergarteners discuss what they've undertaken, cooperate with their classmates, and learn about reading, art, and arithmetic in a meaningful context—not just as an abstraction or a set of exercises on a worksheet page.

The outstanding kindergarten teacher will construct a curriculum that is integrated, well thought out, age appropriate, consistent, and goal oriented.

She Develops a Safe Place for Students to Explore Their Feelings

The excellent kindergarten teacher helps her students use language to express their feelings. She may even set up a learning center that deals exclusively with emotions. For example, such a center might contain ten pictures, each showing a different facial expression. The students would be encouraged to dictate into a tape recorder or to the teacher what they think each picture represents. The ideal kindergarten teacher will also help her students put into words their feelings about stories they have read or movies they have seen. She encourages them to express themselves.

She Teaches Hygiene and Proper Nutrition

Rather than teaching health from posters and books, our exemplary kindergarten teacher will integrate information about cleanliness, dental hygiene, and nutrition into the daily classroom routine. This helps the five-year-olds to take this information personally, rather than seeing it as a "lesson" to be learned. The teacher may also need to assess whether the children are properly clean. You might think this is obvious, but many five-year-olds still have some difficulty in consistently brushing their teeth, wiping their noses, washing their hands, and dressing themselves. She can structure lessons around cleanliness, help the children individually, or meet with their parents to discuss hygiene.

Kindergarten is also a time when the basic building blocks of good nutrition are set down. The ideal kindergarten teacher can talk about food groups and nutrition during weekly cooking lessons, which are always viewed as great fun among kindergarteners. Cooking is an ideal educational activity because it integrates reading (the recipe), math and measurement (for the ingredients), class discussion, and group cooperation.

She Understands the Rhythm of Learning

The outstanding kindergarten teacher will take into account that children's energy levels burst and fade. Quiet time is essential. She will recognize, too, that youngsters who attend afternoon kindergarten sessions may have a different attention span and learning pace than those who are in class at 8:30 A.M. Most kids work better in the morning.

Aimee's teacher, Arla, described to us how she had to alter her morning routine and teaching style after she changed school assignments. At her new placement, children were bused in from many miles away. After a 40-minute ride on a noisy vehicle that jostled its way down the traffic-clogged freeways of Los Angeles, her students were not ready to plunge into learning center activities. They needed some structured, quiet time first to settle down.

The astute kindergarten teacher is sensitive to her students' moods and learning rhythms.

She Uses an Organized System of Discipline

The purpose of discipline should be to teach responsibility and self-reliance, not merely to control the students' behavior. An organized system of discipline will include:

★ Very clear limits and standards about what is and is not acceptable behavior in the classroom and on the playground.

★ A system of consequences that logically fit the infractions. The consequences are presented as choices. (For example, "If you continue to scream, you will take a time-out. The choice is up to you.")

★ Consistent and *calm* follow-through—no screaming or character assassination.

★ An opportunity for the child to discuss with the teacher his part in the misbehavior.

The kindergarten teacher will know how to use time-outs effectively, especially when one child has physically hurt another. A time-out should not be invoked to simply isolate the erring child. Instead, the teacher should send Matthew to the time-out corner with the instruction that he think about the problem and how he contributed to it, and then talk with him about what he would do in the future should the same situation arise. This helps Matthew to express his feelings in words and to take responsibility for his actions.

In some kindergarten classrooms, the time-out is used so effectively that children give themselves a time-out when they feel they are getting out of hand. On a deep level, this indicates their feelings of safety in the classroom.

The great kindergarten teacher will also teach her students what to do in case of conflict. If Randy takes Tanya's crayons, the teacher will have taught the children to use language in order to work out a compromise. If they can't resolve the problem, she has taught them to come to her to help settle the conflict. This is not just tattling or vindictiveness. Rather, the children understand that the teacher will help them in the process of negotiation when the going gets tough.

The Fun Factor

A great kindergarten teacher knows how to make learning fun. Rather than being weighted down with the stilted silence of many children laboriously working over dittoed sheets, her room is filled with the happy and excited sounds of children working and playing together, discovering new information about themselves and their complex world. Music, art, dance, and physical activities are all integrated into the daily routine. It is the kindergarten teacher's responsibility to make learning an enjoyable experience that children will want to pursue for the rest of their lives.

WHAT *NOT* TO EXPECT FROM THE KINDERGARTEN TEACHER

As you can see, being an excellent kindergarten teacher is a tall order. It would be unrealistic to think that your child's teacher can do everything. For example, it is too much to expect that she should communicate to you the moment your child's behavior changes. In the long run, probably at a scheduled conference, she will cover any significant shifts. If you have any concerns or want more frequent progress reports, it's up to you to communicate your needs to her. After all, your child is but one of 25 in the class.

Second, even the most skilled teachers can't supply what's lacking in the home environment. If, for example, you have been unable to assert your will as a parent and maintain adequate discipline with your preschooler, it would be unrealistic to expect that the kindergarten teacher—no matter how good she is—can make up for five years' laxity on your part. It's not her job to turn a whining, demanding, tantrum-throwing child into a paragon of cooperation, sweetness, and light. That's your task. Of course, you can enlist her cooperation and her years of experience to help you.

The effectiveness of any school program is dependent upon reinforcement at home. All the lessons in the world about proper nutrition will fall on deaf ears if you serve your children nothing but fast-food greasy hamburgers and French fries. The teacher can't wash a child's hands in school once a day and expect that she'll remember to do it at home each time she uses the toilet and before meals. These routines must be repeated with you, as well.

That brings us to your responsibility as a parent. The relationship that you create with the school and the teacher also contributes to your child's success in kindergarten. Let's look at what you can do.

YOUR RESPONSIBILITY: COMMUNICATION

In a nutshell, your role is communication, communication, communication—with your child and with the teacher.

In communicating with your child, take her messages seriously. Most children won't complain unless they have a real reason. Pay attention to what Michelle has to say. Sit down and talk with her about how wonderful her day was or about a problem that's bothering her. Then communicate the issues to her teacher—both positive and negative. You can write a note, place a phone call, or set up an appointment.

When Michelle understands that you take her point of view seriously, she feels validated as a person. This increases her feelings of self-esteem. She knows that her happiness is important in your eyes and that you will help her get through a difficult time when necessary.

Ask your child lots of questions. This falls under the heading of encouraging your child to express himself. Don't ask generalizations like "What did you do today?" Most likely you'll get the universal response, "Oh, nothing." Rather, ask leading questions: "How tall was your block tower? Who knocked it down?" It hardly matters that Jason didn't build with blocks today. This still serves to start a conversation with him. If he says, "But I didn't play with blocks," you can reply, "What did you play with?"

Part of your responsibility as a parent is dealing with homework. Should there be homework in your kindergartener's class, it is your responsibility to see that your child completes it and brings it back to school each morning. Homework helps to establish routines and assists children in organizing themselves for learning. If you think about it, homework is also part of the teacher's way of communicating to you about what is going on in the classroom. Take an active interest in your child's homework—but don't do it for him.

This brings us to communicating with the teacher. If there are any—and we mean *any*—changes in your household, you should advise the teacher about them. We're not only referring to major changes like the birth of a sibling, divorce, the parent's loss of a job, or the death of a grandparent. You should also report smaller upheavals in routine, such as an extended visit by Aunt Sally, or a younger brother who has just come down with the chicken pox.

Children are very sensitive to their environment. They react when their routine is tampered with. Often teachers will suspect that something is amiss but may not be able to put their finger on it. Your confirmation will help them deal with your child more effectively.

It's also imperative that you communicate with the teacher about any problems in your child's health or psychological background that could affect his learning. You may balk at such openness, thinking that the teacher may react by attributing every learning or behaviorial issue to your child's "problem." You may fear that she will not even attempt certain activities with your child if she knows of some physical condition. (If, indeed, the teacher responds in that way, you certainly would have good reason to move your child to another class.) A good kindergarten teacher, however, is compassionate. She is able to create a meaningful and sequential way to help your child develop. You can look upon such a teacher as your partner.

Besides communicating problems to the teacher, giving her supportive feedback is the other half of the communication equation. Teachers are people, too. They need a pat on the back once in a while. They need to feel they are doing a good job. When your child is happy in class, let the teacher know. Your input will help make her a better teacher. Otherwise, she may feel taken for granted. Teachers have a tremendous responsibility, and they need your support.

YOUR CHILD HAS A RESPONSIBILITY, TOO

When we asked Aimee's teacher, Arla Capps, what she felt the kindergartener's responsibility is, at first she said simply, "To be a child." On further reflection she added, "Kids are vulnerable. They think that their responsibility is to do what the teacher says. While that's important, I'd also like to see them question the teacher, the environment, and everything around them. I think the child's responsibility is to focus on as many possibilities as he can in one day. He should check everything out."

Then she stopped for a moment and pondered her role as teacher. "You know," she said, "one of my biggest thrills is the chance of getting to that mind at the right moment. The receptivity, the learning process—it's a miracle, in a way."

CHAPTER 10

The Stress Factor: How to Help Your Child Cope

Stress—the very word elicits images of tension headaches. But stress itself is not bad. It is a normal part of life. Any physical or mental action stresses our bodies in some way. In fact, a continuum exists between what psychologists regard as positive or *eu*stress (as in *eu*phoria) and distress (as in, "I'm having a terrible time!").

For us adults, eustress could be the excitement and pleasure that come from buying a new car, getting a promotion, or receiving an A on an exam. Your five-year-old will experience similar elation over adopting a new puppy, enjoying a big birthday party, or just snuggling in your lap and feeling loved. Eustress refers to the high points in life. Those moments are great, but sometimes they are also taxing in their own ways. For example, a job promotion can come with a bigger paycheck and more prestige, but also new and more demanding responsibilities. A puppy, lovable though he is, needs to be fed and housebroken.

Distress, on the other hand, is not just the anxiety and unhappiness experienced when a traumatic event occurs such as illness or death of a parent, divorce, or loss of a job. It is also a relentless day-in and day-out grinding away at the human spirit—a feeling of hopelessness that "things will never get better" when you're stuck at a job you hate and from which you fear you can never escape, or when you feel trapped in a loveless marriage.

Children will feel this sort of distress when their parents are constantly battling or when serious illness strikes at home. School can cause youngsters distress, too.

KINDERGARTEN-INDUCED STRESS

The first day of school has stresses all its own, as your child anticipates how he will do in elementary school. We cover these in the next chapter. For the moment, let's look at situations that can be stressful during the course of kindergarten.

Increased Illness

Anytime your child is exposed to large numbers of new children, she is also exposed to large numbers of new germs. Children who begin preschool seem to try on one another's microbes for size. We remember that when Cherie switched nursery schools after our move, she was sick one week out of each month for about five months. Whatever she brought home traveled around the rest of the family—not a pleasant scenario.

Unfortunately, kindergarten presents much the same problem. Most likely, your child will come into contact with a greater variety of viruses and bacteria in elementary school than ever before. You're dealing with a bigger community.

Illness is stressful because it depletes your child's energy and causes her to miss precious days of school. Short of placing her in quarantine, however, there is not much you can do about it, other than being a stickler for hand washing, nose wiping with tissues (not the backs of hands or sleeves), and the prohibition of sharing food, cups, and straws. We achieved only limited success in these areas, as we could not control what our kids did when they were out of our sight. On the positive side, the frequent illnesses that can occur at the beginning of kindergarten also help to build your child's immunity.

Physical Dangers

The student-to-teacher ratio in kindergarten is much higher than is permissible in preschool, day care, or baby-sitting situations. Teachers are not able to supervise activities as closely in kindergarten as they do for younger children because there are not enough adults to go around. Besides, five-year-olds enjoy a certain measure of independence. They like to experiment with new situations. As a result, elementary school presents your child with more opportunities to get physically hurt.

Again, there is not much you can do about this. Living always carries with it attendant risks. It helps, however, to be aware of the possibilities. If your child expresses some fear for his safety, investigate his anxieties with him and his teacher. If the source of his worry is well founded, talk to the teacher and the school administration, if necessary, to correct the problem.

"Different" Children

In Chapter 2, we mentioned your child's ability to get along with children of varying racial and socioeconomic groups as a part of kindergarten readiness. For children, "different" sometimes translates into "bad" or "frightening." You and the kindergarten teacher should be working toward encouraging your kindergartener's acceptance of all children, no matter what their background.

But "different" can also describe children who are unusually angry or those who have physical disabilities. Your child may fear that she will become the victim of a classmate with a behavior problem, or she may feel her own body image to be threatened by the specter of physical impairment.

Learning how to deal with all children is part of the socialization process. Encourage your preschooler to acknowledge her fears and talk about them. In that way, you can help her to separate reality from her fantasies. In your discussion, you can also teach cause-and-effect ("Monica is angry because her mommy and daddy just had a new baby. Maybe she's feeling left out." "Billy has a cast on his arm because he fell off the jungle gym and got hurt. The cast makes his arm heal better."). With patience and understanding, she will eventually learn how to safely integrate these "different" children into her life.

The World at Large

Once your kindergartener comes into contact with many children, he will be introduced to all kinds of situations that he may have previously been spared. Other children in kindergarten may be stressed because of divorce, illness, death, births, accidents, and other difficult events in their own families. As they act out their stresses or talk about them, your child may also be indirectly affected by them. The situations may be new and frightening to him or the stressed children may become more aggressive as a result of disturbances in their families.

Again, encouraging your child to share his feelings about other children in his world will help him to understand what seems frightening to him and why.

Conflicts with Other Kindergarteners

It is entirely possible that your five-year-old may encounter some difficulty in getting along with one of her classmates. Lisa may come home complaining that Marta is always picking on her. This may cause Lisa some sleepless nights or tummyaches—it may even make her reluctant to go to school in the morning. She just doesn't want to face Marta's scorn.

This is a perfect opportunity to use the kindergarten teacher as a facilitator for socialization issues. By all means, enlist the teacher's assistance. Visit, phone, or write a note to explain your daughter's discomfort. It may be that Marta has been a problem for other children as well. If so, your communication could help mobilize the teacher to seek out the cause and resolution of Marta's negative attitudes. If the problem exists only between the two girls, the teacher can act as a mediator, helping the youngsters to acknowledge and diplomatically resolve their differences.

As a general rule, if your child feels endangered or threatened by other children, let her know that she can always look to a teacher or classroom aide for help. She need not feel alone, since the adults are there to help her with social difficulties.

Teacher's Absence

We all remember instances when our teacher's absence caused our classmates to go berserk—kids popped in and out of their seats, paper airplanes and spitballs zoomed overhead, all semblance of order seemed to evaporate right before our eyes. The poor substitute always had her hands full. Even when the regular teacher returned, the class took a long time to return to normal.

According to child psychoanalyst Erna Furman, teachers sometimes minimize how important they are to children—how much their students' feelings of safety depend on them and how much the kids count on them to be there every day. When kids run amok with a substitute it's not necessarily because the latter can't control the class; rather, the children are upset that their teacher is gone. Addressing teachers in an article on nursery school stress, Ms. Furman writes, "Indeed, we sometimes act as though we expected the children not to notice these changes or not to find them legitimately stressful and difficult to master without our special help."

She suggests that the teacher should prepare her pupils for a planned absence well in advance by talking about the fact that she will be gone and that another teacher will take her place. If a teacher must take time off because of a sudden illness, she may not have the opportunity to warn her class about her absence. In that case, on the day she returns she should spend some time talking with her pupils about why she was absent and should answer pertinent questions posed by the class in order to allay the children's anxiety and stress.

Visitors

Visitors—even those sitting quietly in the back of the room—have a way of distracting kindergarteners and disrupting the daily routine. Certainly you can understand this. You would also feel somewhat suspicious and wary if a stranger came into your office to observe you at work. The kindergarten teacher can dispel some of the stress attached to unfamiliar visitors by introducing them to the class and briefly explaining why they are there. Preparation is the best policy.

Changes in Classroom Set-up

Your kindergartener may view any change in classroom routine as stressful. The rearrangement of furniture, schedules, or activities may overwhelm some five-year-olds. Field trips are fun and educational but can be stressful in much the same way. Again, it is up to the teacher to provide adequate preparation by talking the class through the changes. She can build lessons around these new experiences.

WHEN CONFLICTS OCCUR WITH THE TEACHER

In all of his years as an educator and clinical psychologist, Mitch has discovered that just about everyone has a bad year with a teacher at one time or another during a long and varied school career. We suspect that if you reflect back on your past, you'll come up with some negative experiences as well. In fact, a painful incident in your own past may be motivating your search for the "right" kindergarten placement for your preschooler today.

What causes these conflicts? Sometimes the teaching quality is poor. At other times, the teacher-child relationship just doesn't work and animosity eventually develops in both directions. That can be a sad state of affairs.

Your involvement can help alleviate conflicts. You may need to intervene on your child's behalf by speaking with the teacher or the administrators. Before you begin, you should know that every school system has its own hierarchy. It's important to exhaust each level before moving on to the next. In other words, if your child is having a problem with the teacher, try to work it out with the teacher before going to her superior. You'll only alienate her more if she learns that you have been complaining behind her back. That's human nature. We suggest the following strategy:

★ Conference with the teacher—and if that doesn't work . . .

★ Conference with the counselor (if there is one)—and if that doesn't work . . .

★ Conference with the teacher and the principal together—and if that doesn't work . . .

★ Conference with the principal alone—and if that doesn't work . . .

★ Meeting with the district or area consultant or the school board member for your area.

In setting up a conference, it helps to write a note stating the times when you are available and possible alternatives for phone calls. You don't want to waste your time playing "telephone tag" with one another.

Most often, the situation improves after the air has been cleared. Sometimes, however, you can't correct the problem no matter how hard you try. Our experience with Aimee's third-grade teacher (the one who called her "stupid" in front of the class) is a case in point. This teacher was pregnant. She resigned in the middle of the school year without leaving the replacement teacher a record of her lesson plans or her students' progress. It seems that she just wasn't interested in teaching anymore. Unfortunately, our daughter caught some of the flak.

We held a conference with the teacher and, eventually, with the principal—to little avail. The teacher had her own views about Aimee, and that was that. Interestingly, most of Aimee's classmates were crushed to see this teacher go, but Aimee welcomed the replacement. For her, the new teacher represented a second chance. She and the new teacher were able to develop a warm relationship.

While ours was a rare situation, problems like this do arise from time to time, especially when you feel you have few options. Whatever you do, help your child try to make the best of a difficult predicament. Let her know that she is only responsible for *her* efforts. She can't control the outcome or her teacher's response. Support her efforts wholeheartedly nevertheless. Your child's stress will be diminished when she knows that you're behind her 100 percent.

Together, you need to find a way to get through the year. You might provide enrichment in other areas or extra support. You might interest her in sports or art, providing other outlets for her creativity and new opportunities for garnering a positive self-image.

SO YOUNG, SO MANY STRESSES

It's important for you to view the preceding school-related stresses within the context of your child's more global concerns. Five-year-olds have anxieties and stresses all their own that are separate from school.

Kindergarteners experience a whole range of hurts, slights, and stresses over issues that we as adults may find unimportant—such as not being able to sit next to a best friend during lunch or someone taking a favorite eraser. No matter how seemingly insignificant to you, your child's stresses are important to him and warrant your attention.

The following are a few rather extreme but common examples of situations that can cause children to become distraught and upset.

★ Mother's pregnancy and the birth of a sibling or half-sibling.

★ Your marital problems and the child's fantasies about the possible dissolution of the family.

★ Your remarriage and the child's integration into a new, blended family.

★ Their own illness or yours.

★ Conflicts with friends.

★ Loss or forced relinquishing of a transitional object such as a "blankie" or special stuffed animal, coupled with the parental attitude of "you're a big boy now, you don't need this."

★ Overscheduling with little off-time.

★ Understimulation (children whose parents don't take the time to plan for them feel rejected and alone).

★ Performance anxieties ("Will I be good enough?").

★ Unrealistic parental expectations: having to be the "perfect" child.

★ A death in the family, including the death of a beloved pet.

★ A move from one home to another or from one town to another.

★ Vacation travel and unfamiliar, frequently changing sleeping arrangements.

★ Your frequent absence because of job-related demands.

★ Your sudden return to work when you have spent the last few years at home in a child-care capacity.

★ Any kind of physical, psychological, or sexual abuse.

As you can see, many of these stresses revolve around your five-year-old's lack of control over his environment. In fact, he may have very little control over your marriage or other familial concerns. If things aren't going well for you and the rest of the family, he most certainly will be affected by it.

HOME-RELATED STRESS

Children are very perceptive. When you are distressed, they will pick up on your feelings, and your unhappiness is upsetting to them. We remember an incident years ago when our daughter Cherie was still a baby. One day the two of us adults had an argument in the front seat of the car while Cherie sat contentedly in her car seat behind us. After about three minutes of our yelling at one another, Cherie joined in with wails of her own. Although she most certainly didn't understand what we were saying, she did read our emotions correctly. We were angry and that was frightening and distressing to her.

If you as a couple argue all the time, if you are caught up in the care of an aging and chronically or acutely ill parent, if you are frantically working two jobs just to make ends meet, your child will experience the fallout. Your stress is stressful to her as well.

Keep in mind especially that when times are hard for you, you may not have a lot of energy to give to your children. You may withdraw into your own world to lick your wounds. You may even expect, on some unconscious level, your youngster to take care of you by not bothering you with her normal demands or by actually taking over adult roles in the household. Besides, you may perceive her childlike needs as unimportant compared to yours. You are not available in the same capacity as you used to be, and your child can experience your reactions as abandonment.

In addition, if you are recently separated from your spouse, you may turn to your child to help fill your loneliness, inappropriately using her as a friend and confidante. Your confessions and anger over the situation can only further confuse a five-year-old who is still trying to understand why her world is suddenly torn asunder. Unfortunately, most young children assume that any death or divorce in the family must be their fault. They feel they must do something to remedy the situation—which, of course, is impossible. This helplessness in itself can be stressful.

HOW STRESS AFFECTS KINDERGARTEN PERFORMANCE AND SELF-ESTEEM

Unfortunately, when families are having problems, children suffer, too. Your five-year-old has a limited attention span as it is. Whether he worries about the state of your marriage, the health of his pet gerbil, or the fact that his best friend is already doing subtraction, Sean will be distracted from his school activities when he is distressed. As he thinks about these problems, he doesn't concentrate on the subject at hand—addition facts or vowel sounds. Gaps develop in his learning.

Kindergarten sets down the basic building blocks of your child's education. Each element is dependent upon the next. If the stress lasts for a long time, Sean's educational gaps widen. It becomes a vicious cycle. The less he pays attention, the less he learns. When he does check in to see what the class is up to, he can be totally lost.

Such distractions can lead to your child's being labeled "slow" or an "underachiever." He may hear your angry voice asking, "Why don't you get this? It's so easy." His self-esteem is called into question. Sean may feel stupid, but in reality he is distracted by the stress in the family.

Because of the potential learning problems that chronic distress can evoke, it is essential for you to recognize when your child is suffering distress.

SIGNS OF DISTRESS IN YOUNG CHILDREN

Some children have a hard time putting their feelings into words. They may not tell you that they are upset. Some five-year-olds will act our their unhappy emotions; others simply withdraw and clam up. It's up to you, then, to pay close attention to your child's behavior. This may be difficult if you're so caught up in your own painful situation that you don't have the wherewithal to cope with your child's plight. Yet, it's important to bear in mind that nipping small problems in the bud averts larger problems later.

A word of caution: persistent headaches, stomachaches, or any other continuing physiological symptoms should be investigated by the appropriate physician.

Your child is letting you know in subtle and not so subtle ways that she is feeling school- or home-induced stress if she experiences *any* of the following:

★ Sleep disturbances
    waking up in the middle of the night
    nightmares and night terrors
    sudden difficulty falling asleep
    somnambulism (sleepwalking) in severe cases

★ Eating disturbances
    sudden loss of appetite
    overeating
    frequent stomachaches, nausea, or diarrhea
    (when physical causes have been ruled out)

★ Frequent physical complaints such as headaches

★ Hyperactivity or unusual tiredness

★ Boredom (psychologists often view boredom in children as a precursor of depression)

★ Aggressiveness toward other children or with toys and pets

★ Inappropriate or sexualized play with dolls

★ Dark, angry, or violent drawings using primarily the colors black and red

★ Drawings in which family members are represented as disproportionately large or small

★ Repetitive, ritualized behavior such as chewing the corner of the blanket, stroking a toy, or twirling a strand of hair

★ Clinginess

★ Whininess

★ Regressive behavior such as bed-wetting and thumb-sucking

★ Withdrawal from normal family interactions

★ Frequent, unwarranted temper tantrums
★ Accident-prone behavior and personal injury

Many of these behaviors in children are a cry for help. The rule of thumb: Any behavior that is unusual or an extreme change should be investigated as a sign of stress.

HOW TO DEAL WITH YOUR CHILD'S STRESS

For the last several years, as part of his psychology practice, Mitch has worked at the Wellness Community in Santa Monica, California. There he has counseled thousands of cancer patients, helping them to reduce the stress they feel as a result of their illness and their lives in general. From his training and work at the Wellness Community, Mitch has found that the most useful tenets of stress reduction include communication, relaxation, and visualization.

You can apply these three principles to help diffuse your child's unhappiness when he feels stressed. It might be helpful to think of the exercises below as you would physical training. Your child needs to know how to swim one lap before he can join a swim team. Likewise, these short-term stress-reducers have long-term implications. When used consistently and over time they provide a way to effectively deal with stressful events.

Another word of caution: If your child refuses to go along with the exercises or if none of them alleviates his stress—and especially if you suspect some kind of child abuse from an outside source—you would be well-advised to seek assistance from the school and even professional counseling. A psychologist can help you figure out the family system that is perpetuating the stressful situations. The time and expense are well worth it. It is easier to deal with an unhappy five-year-old than with a sullen and rebellious teenager who has been nursing an assortment of hurts for a decade or more.

Communication

Children may feel stressed when they have little control over a family situation. Helping youngsters gain a bit of control over their lives serves to manage some of their distress.

If Josh is tired in the morning, for example, and has difficulty rolling out of bed and getting ready for school, it may help for both of you to talk about how his father's longer work hours now mean that he must stay up late just to see dad. In the discussion, a solution may emerge that entails a shift in dad's work day (can he begin an hour earlier and end an hour earlier?), a mental-health day off for dad once in a while, or the commitment to spend special time together during the weekend.

Sometimes, in truth, there is not much the child can do about the troubling situation—especially in cases of death or divorce. Children's natural egocentrism leads them to blame themselves for the family disaster. Just being able to talk about how difficult times have become can help. Sometimes it's useful to get counseling, even if only for a few sessions—especially if your child's behavior has changed dramatically.

However, as child developmentalist Dr. David Elkind so wisely points out in his book *The Hurried Child: Growing Up Too Fast Too Soon*, sending the child off to a therapist by himself may reinforce his feelings that the divorce was his fault—that he is the "sick" one who needs treatment. Dr. Elkind advises that when marriage breaks down and therapy is an option, at least one parent should accompany the youngster to the sessions.

In our family, when we run into rocky moments, we call for a family meeting. Family meetings are specific times we set aside to deal with mutual concerns. One parent usually convenes a meeting whenever a family member—parent or child—is uncharacteristically out of sorts. During a family meeting we suspend all traditional roles. Each member has the opportunity to speak his or her mind without interruption. We share our concerns honestly. Afterwards we feel that the others have heard our needs, even if we can't fully resolve them. A family meeting can help your kindergartener gain a sense of power and control over his life within a context that is acceptable to you.

Family meetings are also important because they help your five-year-old take responsibility for his actions. If he is exhibiting signs of distress, you can say, "Alan, I've noticed how rough you're playing with your toys. I found your G.I. Joe broken in the yard. Are you angry or upset about something? Help me to understand what's going on with you." This kind of question encourages your son to define and assess his behavior. It gives him the freedom to express his emotions in words. In addition, he can discover from your interaction that his words and feelings make an impact on you. You may even be willing to change situations to suit his needs. That can improve his feelings of self-esteem.

Encourage your five-year-old to use language to ask for what she wants. If Mara is upset about moving, she may be expressing her anxiety and emotional pain by wetting her bed at night. During a family meeting, rather than yelling at her for acting like a baby, ask her what is going on. She may respond by telling you that she never wants to leave her old house. You can then interpret her bed-wetting as a wish to hang on to her childhood security.

While you can't reverse your plans to move, you may mitigate your daughter's unhappiness by coming up with a plan. You can say, "I know you don't want to move, but unfortunately, that's not up to you. Is there anything we can do to help you with your feelings about it?"

Mara may respond that she wants to take the house with her. In that case, you can promise (and then follow through, of course) to take lots of pictures of the inside and outside of the house so that she can look at them whenever she feels that she misses her old environment. That's a symbolic way of taking the house with her. If you're moving within the same city, you can also make monthly trips to see how the old house is faring. Eventually, as Mara becomes acclimated to her new surroundings, she will let go of the old neighborhood.

The key here, however, is for Mara to let you know what she is feeling. You may be able to elicit that by merely asking questions like, "How do you feel about our moving?" Be prepared for her negative response. Jumping in with comments about how wonderful your new residence will be ("You'll have your own room and a big yard and swings.") may not assuage her sorrow over losing her childhood home. Rather, you can empathize with her feelings by reiterating that it must be difficult for her and that it's OK for her to be sad about moving.

Our family meetings are usually somewhat structured. It may seem silly to make a discussion among family members so formal. After all, we do see one another every day and we talk about things in passing. But some issues warrant special time—especially if you perceive that your child is distressed. Calling for a family meeting means that you're all making a commitment to be involved and to deal with specific issues. The following are some guidelines to help you organize your meetings:

1. *Set up a specific time and place.* Establish the time in advance, either by creating a regular weekly meeting time or by designating a future time. In that way, all family members will be sure to attend. Find a quiet environment where you won't be interrupted.

Hold your phone calls. You're sending your kindergartener the message that family communication is *important*.

2. *Limit the time of the meeting.* Nothing is worse than a discussion going on for hours and hours. Depending on your child's attention span, meetings can run from 15 minutes to an hour. A time limit helps keep the meeting contained and promotes the feeling of safety.

3. *Cover a specific topic.* You might call a meeting to discuss Mara's unhappiness about moving, for example. Don't confuse issues by bringing in your dissatisfaction about the way she has been cleaning her room lately or how she just ruined her brand new socks. A single-issue meeting helps your family to focus. The clearer focus you have, the more likely you'll be to find some kind of resolution. It's easier to juggle one problem than five.

4. *Give each person his fair turn.* In order for the meeting to work properly, each family member deserves the time to express himself, to be heard and understood. Allow enough time for everyone. Each of your perspectives is valuable.

5. *Allow the problem to go unresolved, if necessary.* Sometimes it's impossible to come up with a solution to a problem in the moment. You may feel frustrated if you believe you must resolve the issue *today*. When you "sleep on" a problem, however, you may come up with a more creative solution. Feel free to schedule follow-up meetings if you reach an impasse. By limiting time and setting up several meetings, you enhance the creative process.

6. *Use good communication skills.* In Chapter 6 we discussed communication skills such as getting down to your child's level, really listening, making eye contact, and using puppets to enhance family conversations. These skills are equally applicable during family meetings. To those, we'd like to add a few more.

For example, it's important for you to ask questions in non-threatening ways. If you approach Mara's bed-wetting with questions like, "What's wrong with you? Aren't you ashamed of yourself? Aren't you ever going to grow up? When are you going to stop peeing in your bed?" she is not likely to open up to you. In fact, she will be more apt to react angrily or withdraw further into her shell. That's not the desired result. Rather, your question should be phrased somewhat like this: "I notice that your bed has been wet. What do you think is happening? Our family has been under a lot of stress. Is it affecting you?"

Another useful skill is *mirroring*. This is a way to validate your child's feelings. When you mirror your child's feelings you communicate to her that you understand what is bothering her, with statements such as, "I know moving must be hard for you. You feel sad about leaving this house, don't you?" This will go a long way in establishing trust and allowing Mara's feelings to surface.

7. *Express love.* This is probably the most important part of the meeting! We never end our meetings without some show of affection for each other, even if we have vented angry or frustrated feelings during our talk. When family meetings end with hugs and kisses all around, they are a great way to let your youngster know that you love him and stand by him, no matter what. That in itself can help to relieve stress.

Relaxation

Relaxation exercises help to relieve stress for children and adults alike. Mitch has found the following exercises successful in helping to relax the children whom he sees in his practice. Kids usually go along with them willingly. In fact, these exercises are good for parents, too. Parents may find the tone of their voice changing as they lead their youngsters through the steps, because they become relaxed as well. In truth, these exercises are a wonderful way of spending quality time together. You might want to call the exercise the "Relaxation Game."

1. *Teach deep breathing.* Have your child lie down on the floor or bed. You can lie down beside him. Ask him to pretend that there is a straw running from his mouth to his belly button. Tell him to think of his belly button as the opening of a balloon. Each time he breathes deeply, the balloon fills up with air. When he exhales, the balloon collapses. Continue deep breathing for two to three minutes.

2. *Ease tension.* Ask your child where in his body he feels tense: head, neck, shoulders, or back. Ask him to "breathe" into that area. Repeat to him that with each breath he takes, his neck is getting more relaxed and warmer.

Some children like an alternate exercise of tensing the already tense muscle for a count of ten and then relaxing it. Then do three to five repetitions.

A third possibility is to relax the whole body. Beginning with your child's toes, tell him to tense his feet and then relax them. Next, go to his calves and thighs. Work your way up his body, going from the chest to the neck and head. Finish with the neck, shoulders, and arms. As each area is relaxed, tell your child that it feels heavy, as if it's sinking to the ground. Once you reach the fingertips, have him imagine that all the tension is flowing out of his fingers into the ground.

Visualization

Once you're all nice and relaxed, you might try a visualization exercise. Visualization reduces stress by transforming negative experiences or difficulties into positive images. You imagine a wonderfully pleasant scene and then carry through by fantasizing the resolution to a problem in that scene.

For visualization to be most effective, your child should be in a relaxed state. All the while, remind her to breathe gently in and out. Talking in a soft and steady voice, suggest to your youngster that she choose her favorite place—somewhere she feels happy, secure, comforted, and safe. It could be at Disneyland, floating on still blue waters, in bed with a cuddly blanket, or in your arms. She need not tell you what she's experiencing. In fact, don't interrupt the visualization with conversation. Just let her fantasize anything she wants.

Next ask her to imagine that she is walking toward this favorite place. When she gets there she'll choose a spot that is all hers. Have her imagine that she is lying down in this spot and that she feels warm, safe, and comfortable there. She feels nothing but positive energy.

If your child has been suffering from a headache, you can help to relieve the tension by asking her to imagine the headache going into a box that she closes tightly with a lid. Then tell her to see the box getting smaller and smaller until it floats away, out of her body. If she experiences pain elsewhere in her body, you can ask her to imagine the pain as an object that has shape and color. Then she can visualize the object transforming into something clearer and lighter that simply floats away.

Once your child has had some time to experience this form of stress reduction, you can then ask her to imagine that she is leaving her spot and coming home. Add the suggestion that she feels rested, relaxed, and happy inside. As she emerges from the tranquil state, remind her that she is now wide awake, alert, clearheaded—and feeling much better.

Although stress is an inevitable part of the school experience, dealing with both school-induced stress and life-induced stress that affects school performance will prepare your child for some of the rough-and-tumble of the grown-up world. It's important to learn that times can be difficult but still we survive. That's a painful piece of information, but one that can serve your child well throughout her lifetime.

CHAPTER 11

Tears of Sorrow, Tears of Joy: Preparing for the First Day

What an exciting morning it was. Our younger daughter, Aimee, was about to enter kindergarten . . . at last. All those years of anticipation, all those moments with her face pressed against the schoolyard gate watching wide-eyed as her older sister played, yearning to be a part of the "big kids'" world—these would now all come to fruition. Our baby was starting school.

Externally, Susan had been preparing Aimee and herself for weeks. There were the requisite school shopping trips, the new shoes and Snoopy lunch box, and the school registration one very hot day in late August when all of the official papers had to be filled out and proof given of immunizations and district residence. These had taken place with a certain sense of calm. Aimee was our second child. We had done this before. There were to be no great surprises.

Besides, Susan asked herself, how different could this be from nursery school? It was not as if Aimee had been with her mother 24 hours a day. She had friends, she was interested in what went on around her. True, she was a bit disorganized—but she was young for her grade. She'd grow out of it.

In truth, however, Susan had not fully prepared herself internally. Kindergarten *is* different from preschool. According to Erna Furman, an early-childhood educator and child psychoanalyst, "The idea of entering public school is apt to make parents [and] children . . . a bit anxious. The step implies showing oneself to the world, letting society judge whether one amounts to something. The children worry whether they will be adequate to the demands of the 'big' school; the parents worry how their child's behavior will reflect on their parenting."

For the moment, our family had pushed those anxieties aside. We finished breakfast and got dressed. After a kiss and hug from Mitch, Susan and Aimee went across the street to pick up Aimee's best friend, Ali, along with her mom.

The four of them walked the familiar blocks to school, the girls alternately speeding ahead, jumping up and down with excitement, and then stopping to wait for the moms to catch up or to cross the busy streets. Once in the school auditorium, they sat side by side in the agitated buzz. About 100 children and parents anxiously fidgeted in the cavernous room, all waiting for the big moment.

The principal stood before the group, welcomed everyone to school and introduced the teachers. Then he slowly called the children's names in alphabetical order. One by one the five-year-olds took leave of their parents.

"Alix Friedberg. Room 7. Mrs. Capps." Ali disengaged herself from Aimee and marched bravely up to the front of the auditorium and put herself in the proper line.

We were not far behind. "Aimee Golant." Susan could feel Aimee's body stiffen in anticipation. "Room 7. Mrs. Capps." Aimee let out a squeal of joy and bolted from Susan's side, barely giving her mom a kiss or a backward glance. Susan knew why. After three years of attending different nursery schools, Aimee and Ali were finally united in the same institution, in the same room, with the same teacher. They could barely contain their elation. The two five-year-olds stood up at the front of the auditorium hugging each other in utter bliss as the other names were called.

Now, even though she had no more reason to stay, Susan could not bring herself to leave. She was satisfied with Aimee's class placement. It was unnecessary for her to watch until all of the children had been summoned to the front of the room. Yet, she sat in that room (so reminiscent of her own elementary school) as if bolted to her folding chair—and wept.

"This is it," she thought. "It's over. My baby is gone. I know now how my mother felt when I started kindergarten." As she watched those 40 little heads line up and walk out of the auditorium into the *big* school with all of the *big* kids, her tears turned into exaltation. "This is it," she thrilled. "It's over. My baby is growing up."

A TIME OF MIXED FEELINGS FOR PARENTS

The first day of kindergarten is indeed a time of mixed feelings. As parents, we often experience some measure of relief and certainly joy. "Whew! We made it this far. What a great day!" Or, as Susan was certainly feeling, "I'm free!"

Yet there are also attendant anxieties:

★ Were we adequate parents?

★ Will our child succeed or at least do OK?

★ Will he make friends?

★ Will he feel as if he belongs?

★ Will he get along with the teacher?

★ Was his preschool preparation solid?

★ Will what he learned in preschool complement the curriculum at kindergarten?

★ Will he feel safe here?

★ Will he grow and thrive?

★ Will this school match our child's needs?

★ What am I going to do with my life, now that I'm no longer a full-time mother?

One family who came to Mitch's psychology practice for counseling was worried about their daughter's upcoming kindergarten experience. Caroline had been enrolled in a Montessori-type school, a highly structured environment that stressed academics. Marge and Ken were concerned that the kindergarten at their local public school would be too diffuse. They feared that Caroline would not get enough attention, even though most states (and theirs in particular) mandate small teacher-student ratios for kindergarten. No matter how reassuring the facts were, Ken and Marge's fears would not be assuaged.

For this couple, the issue was letting go of the control they had had while their daughter was in nursery school. They realized, painfully, that they could not remain in charge of all that Caroline would now experience. This feeling of helplessness evoked upsetting memories for both of them—memories of being teased, of being excluded from the "in" groups, of feeling intimidated by the older children in the schoolyard and the hallways, of falling down and getting hurt, of hearing other teachers yelling in frighteningly loud voices at their classrooms of older children. They displaced these difficult memories from their own childhoods onto their daughter.

Indeed, each of us has painful memories of kindergarten experiences. Mitch remembers how his teacher ridiculed him in front of the class. It was Valentine's Day and the class was making hearts for their mothers out of lace doilies and red construction paper. Mitch wasn't as dexterous as his peers—he is left-handed and the scissors were designed for right-handed people. His teacher snatched his project out of his hands to show the class how *not* to make a valentine. As she corrected the clumsiness of his work, he was left with a perfect valentine but a broken heart. He felt that he just wasn't good enough. Deep in his heart, he knew that the gift he offered to his mom (and which she accepted with such joy) was a fraud—it was not truly the work of his own hands.

Susan had an equally embarrassing experience. She had developed an all-consuming crush on one of her classmates, Michael. Too shy to approach him directly, she resigned herself to worshiping him from afar. Then one day by chance he sat down next to her during the story circle. Her excitement knew no bounds. Unfortunately, neither did her bladder. Unable to contain herself and unwilling to excuse herself for fear of losing her seat next to her beloved, she had an accident right then and there. She never was able to face Michael again.

Often we carry over our experiences from childhood into the parenting of our children. In a sense we relive our own pasts as we marshal our kids through the various stages they must encounter as they grow. At each turn in the road, we remember how it was for us. Sometimes, as in the case of Marge and Ken, we act out of our own fears rather than assessing what's really happening with our kids.

Talking to our children about our own experiences in a supportive and encouraging way helps to defuse some of our anxiety. In addition, the sharing of our past helps to let our youngsters know that they're not alone in their fears—everyone goes through these experiences. Of course, that doesn't mean we should overwhelm our five-year-olds with the gory details. But we can share some of the funnier stories in an attempt to clarify in our own minds which experiences belong to our past and which belong to our children.

SEPARATION CAN BE HARD ON MOM AND DAD

Fear of separation often underlies our anxieties. Yet frequently we focus only on our preschooler's separation anxieties. Will she cry once we leave her at kindergarten? Will she retreat into a corner and suck her thumb? Few of us consider that parents may suffer from separation anxiety, too. Susan certainly felt the tug when Aimee ran toward her future with such gay abandon. It was as if a piece of Susan were suddenly flying off into the wind, never to be recaptured. Aimee didn't seem to give it a second thought.

In her excellent essay on readiness for kindergarten, nursery school director and psychoanalyst Erna Furman elaborates on this issue:

> A change in the child is accompanied by an inevitable change in the mother-child relationship. Mothers have an inkling that the child's entry into public school coincides more or less with a big developmental step. The unique emotional closeness with mother, so characteristic of the preschool years, gives way to a relative withdrawal. . . . The child forges ahead, the parents are left behind.

Fathers have their own particular brand of separation anxiety. From Mitch's many years of working with men in his "Finding Time for Fathering" seminars, he has found that dads fear for their youngsters' safety when they begin kindergarten. Men sense that their children are coming into contact with the "outside world," and on some level they feel powerless to prevent dangerous situations from occurring.

According to Ms. Furman, the step into kindergarten also diminishes closeness between mother and child. You may experience this as a profound loss. When Jonathan began preschool, you were still fully involved in every intimate detail of his daily care; but Jonathan-the-kindergartener will now begin focusing on others—his teacher and his peers—for social, emotional, and intellectual contact. That is as it should be.

Yet, these feelings of anxiety and abandonment can be painful for you. You may not recognize the source of your uneasiness. After all, you may feel that you should celebrate your child's achievement of this milestone. Still, you feel fear, sadness, and loss. There may be a part of you that just doesn't want your child to grow up. You may even be unconsciously communicating your ambivalence to your youngster with statements such as, "You'll be fine, won't you?" instead of more positive affirmations such as, "I know you'll be fine!"

Take a moment, then, to consider what it means to you that your child is starting kindergarten. Are you feeling OK about it? Just recognizing that this is a complex time, filled with both the joy and pain of growing up, can go a long way in helping you cope with your emotions. In truth, getting your child ready for kindergarten also means preparing yourself.

YOUR PRESCHOOLER FEELS ANXIOUS, TOO

Of course, parents aren't the only ones to experience anxiety before kindergarten. Your child may also ask himself a myriad of questions:

★ Will I be smart or grown up enough?

★ Will the other kids like me?

★ Will I make friends?

★ Will my teacher be mean or nice?

★ Will everyone find out that I don't know the whole alphabet yet? Will they laugh at me?

★ What if I get lost in the halls or can't find the bathroom? It's such a big place!

★ What if I'm scared of the playground?

★ What if I can't handle kindergarten? It's all so big and new and different!

Your child will communicate his underlying needs to you somehow. As we discussed in the previous chapter, his anxiety may come out in many different ways. Your task is to listen and be supportive. Remember, children can tolerate a certain amount of anxiety, as long as it doesn't overwhelm them.

WAYS TO ADDRESS YOUR FIVE-YEAR-OLD'S FEARS

What if your child suddenly regresses and behaves childishly as if to forestall the inevitable? In that case, you may find it helpful to engage him in a conversation about his fears. Ask him if he has any thoughts about starting kindergarten. How does he feel about it? Don't deny his expressions of anxiety with words such as, "You're a big boy now. You shouldn't feel that way." Instead, just listen to what's on his mind. Use the mirroring techniques that we suggest in the previous chapter. They will help to validate his feelings.

You'll probably find that your five-year-old is experiencing a sense of loss, too. Entering kindergarten may mean that Marissa is leaving a group of friends, a teacher, and a preschool, a day-care setting, or home, where she has spent a good many hours of her young life. She may miss the old, comfortable environment in which she has felt secure and loved. This is natural. Yet, adjusting to change is a part of growing up.

Reassure your daughter about her loss: "I know it's hard for you to say good-bye to your teacher at the play school." As we suggest in the previous chapter, taking lots of photographs helps mitigate the loss, much as it would if you were moving. For your preschooler, changing schools is a loss similar in scope to changing homes. If time permits, you can even establish a loose schedule of contact with the old environment, so that Marissa doesn't feel it's entirely out of her reach. Eventually, she'll outgrow the need to return.

On the other hand, you may find that your five-year-old is very excited about the impending change. Kids have a biological need to learn. They look forward to new situations and growth. The first day of kindergarten is the culmination of years of experience. It can be a moment of great exhilaration.

As you can see, you and your children have many complex feelings about this big step. Give yourselves the opportunity to sort out your emotions, and by all means enlist the help of the preschool teacher. Share your concerns and ask her how other families cope with the transition. Most likely she has traveled this road many times before and her advice can be encouraging and helpful. Besides, she too may be experiencing some anxiety and loss as the "succeeding generations" of her charges move out into the world.

OTHER WAYS TO MAKE THE TRANSITION A POSITIVE EXPERIENCE

You can impart a feeling of excitement about the first day of kindergarten by being excited yourself. Your expressions can help create a positive attitude toward learning:

★ "Look how you've grown!"
★ "The world is opening up for you!"
★ "You can be anything you want to be!"
★ "Kindergarten is the first giant step!"

On the other hand, it's important not to use kindergarten as a threat. Statements like, "When you get to kindergarten, your teacher won't let you do that," or "All the children in kindergarten will laugh at you if you suck your thumb," may create feelings of dread or apprehension. Avoid these.

Another good way to create positive feelings about school is to read lots of stories about the first day at kindergarten. Some are fun while others are quite informative (see References and Suggested Reading). Books, coupled with a classroom visit, help to reduce your child's fear of the unknown.

SHOULD YOU SPEND THE FIRST DAY WITH YOUR CHILD?

Most kindergarten teachers do not recommend that you stay with your five-year-old for the first day. Your presence can be a distraction to your child and to the other students in the classroom and can make the entire separation process more difficult. Some children, especially those who have had little prior preschool experience or those who have stayed at home with a baby-sitter, may need more reassurance. You can say, "It's time now for all of the mommies to leave and I have to leave, too. But I know that you'll do just fine. I'll be here waiting for you when school is over."

Your youngster's adjustment can be eased by having a buddy in the class. If you haven't done this yet, you may want to encourage your youngster to cultivate friendships with other children who will attend the same school. In that way, she won't feel all alone once you leave.

What if your five-year-old cries and carries on? While you may feel embarrassed by the scene, rest assured that you are not throwing her to the lions by leaving her at school. Some of her tears may be fueled by her desire to impress or manipulate you, or she may truly be upset about the prospect of school. Some children cry because they sense their parents' anxiety.

In any case, most teachers recommend that you do not stay despite the tears, although you may be allowed a few extra minutes to get your child settled. You can even promise a special after-school adventure. You'll find, however, that once you leave the classsroom, your child may cry for a few minutes longer but soon she will stop, surrendering to her fascination with the new surroundings, classmates, and activities.

"ALL I REALLY NEED TO KNOW
I LEARNED IN KINDERGARTEN"

By now, we're sure you've heard of or read Robert Fulghum's clever and wise book about life and the kindergarten sandbox, *All I Really Need to Know I Learned in Kindergarten*. It goes, in part, as follows:

> Most of what I really need to know about how to live, and what to do and how to be, I learned in kindergarten. . . . These are the things I learned: Share everything. Play fair. Clean up your own mess. Don't take things that aren't yours. Say you're sorry when you hurt somebody. Wash your hands before you eat. Flush. Warm cookies and milk are good for you. Live a balanced life. Learn some and think some and draw and paint and sing and dance and play and work every day some.

Would that life were so simple. Yet, in looking back on our own kindergarten experiences and those of our children, we also came up with some profound insights.

Mitch, for example, came to recognize the power of his imagination during his year in kindergarten. He remembers that during the reading of *Raggedy Ann and Andy* he suddenly realized that he could picture the action in his mind. He was thrilled at the idea that the world of the mind and the imagination had opened up to him.

Susan learned about limits and boundaries. Her kindergarten teacher explained to the class about why it was important to draw an outline around a figure. The teacher demonstrated by painting eyes, nose, and mouth without benefit of the outline of the face, and shirt stripes without delineating the shape of the body. Susan understood from this, on some level that she could certainly not verbalize at the time, how important it was for the self to be contained within boundaries.

Cherie describes how she learned that different people could be good at different activities. Her kindergarten class was given the honor of painting a mural on the wall of the schoolyard with the help of a local artists' group. While Cherie painted her tree with flowers, her best friend made a very elaborate house. The supervising artist became excited by the house, praised it, and helped Lara to complete it. Cherie felt jealous about the attention her friend received.

The next part of the project, however, was for each child to dictate a story about what she had painted. When Cherie's teacher loved her story, our five-year-old understood that although she might not be as good an artist as Lara, she was a great storyteller.

Aimee recalls learning that kids aren't always nice. During story time one day she started to sit beside Ali on the rug. Just as she was lowering her body, Rebecca scooted into her spot from behind.

"I was going to sit there," Aimee declared.

"Well, I was here first and three's a crowd," Rebecca replied, giggling at her own cunning.

Not wanting to make a fuss, Aimee sat beside Rebecca, the other seat next to Ali having long been occupied. But she and Rebecca never did get along well after that.

Why are we sharing these family stories with you? Because kindergarten is a significant transition for your child. He will learn important lessons there, many of which have little to do with academics. In truth, by getting your child ready for kindergarten, you are also preparing him for life.

References and Suggested Reading

ALLEN, K. EILEEN, and ELIZABETH M. GOETZ, editors. *Early Childhood Education: Special Problems, Special Solutions.* Rockville, Md.: Aspen Systems Corporation, 1982.

ANASTASI, ANNA. *Psychological Testing.* Sixth edition. New York: Macmillan Publishing Co., 1988.

BREDEKAMP, SUE, and LORRIE SHEPARD. "How Best to Protect Children from Inappropriate School Expectations, Practices, and Policies." *Young Children* 44 (March 1989): 14–24.

CARMODY, DEIRDRE. "Debate Intensifying on Screening Tests before Kindergarten." *New York Times*, May 11, 1989.

CHARLESWORTH, ROSALIND. "Behind before They Start: Deciding How to Deal with the Risk of Kindergarten 'Failure.'" *Young Children* 44 (March 1989): 5–13.

ELKIND, DAVID. "Early Childhood Education on Its Own Terms." In *Early Schooling: The National Debate*, edited by Sharon L. Kagan and Edward F. Zigler. New Haven: Yale University Press, 1987.

_____ . *The Hurried Child: Growing Up Too Fast Too Soon.* Revised Edition. Reading, Mass.: Addison-Wesley, 1988.

_____ . *Miseducation: Preschoolers at Risk.* New York: Knopf, 1987.

FISHER, KATHLEEN. "Pushing Preschoolers Doesn't Help, May Hurt." *The APA Monitor* 20 (July 1989): 9.

FISKE, EDWARD B. "Choice of Public Schools May Be Wave of Future." *The New York Times*, June 4, 1989.

FURMAN, ERNA. "Readiness for Kindergarten" and "Stress in the Nursery School." In *What Nursery School Teachers Ask Us About: Psychoanalytic Consultations in Preschool; Emotions and Behavior Monographs* No. 5, edited by Erna Furman. Madison, Conn.: International Universities Press, 1986.

GOLANT, MITCH, with BOB CRANE. *It's OK to Be Shy!* New York: TOR Books, 1987.

————. *Sometimes It's OK to Be Angry!* New York: TOR Books, 1987.

GOLANT, MITCH, and SUSAN GOLANT. *Disciplining Your Preschooler and Feeling Good About It.* Los Angeles: Lowell House, 1989.

HOFFMAN, LOIS W. "Effects of Maternal Employment on Two-Parent Families." *American Psychologist* 44 (February 1989): 283–292.

JONES, RUSSELL A., CLYDE HENDRICK, and YACOV M. EPSTEIN. *Introduction to Social Psychology.* Sunderland, Mass.: Sinauer Associates, Inc., 1979.

KANTROWITZ, BARBARA, and PAT WINGERT. "How Kids Learn." *Newsweek* 113 (April 17, 1989): 50–57.

KATZ, LILIAN G. "Early Education: What Should Young Children Be Doing?" In *Early Schooling: The National Debate*, edited by Sharon L. Kagan and Edward F. Zigler. New Haven: Yale University Press, 1987.

KRANYIK, MARGERY. *Starting School: How to Help Your Three- to Eight-Year-Old Make the Most of School.* New York: Continuum, 1982.

KUTNER, LAWRENCE. "Parent & Child: The Best Way to Help Rejected Children Gain Acceptance Is to Teach Them New Social Skills." *New York Times*, December 22, 1988.

LANGER, P., J. M. KALK, and D. T. SEARLS. "Age of Admission and Trends in Achievement: A Comparison of Blacks and Caucasians." *American Educational Research Journal* 21 (1984): 61–78.

LUDINGTON-HOE, SUSAN, with SUSAN K. GOLANT. *How to Have a Smarter Baby.* New York: Bantam Books, 1987.

MEISELS, S. J. "Uses and Abuses of Developmental Screening and School Readiness Tests." *Young Children* 42 (1987): 4–6, 68–73.

NATIONAL ASSOCIATION FOR THE EDUCATION OF YOUNG CHILDREN. *Appropriate Education in the Primary Grades: A Position Statement.* Washington, D.C.: NAEYC #578, 1988.

_____ . *Good Teaching Practices for 4- and 5-Year Olds: A Position Statement.* Washington, D.C.: NAEYC #522, 1986.

O'CONNOR, JOHN J. "What Are Commercials Selling to Children?" *New York Times,* June 6, 1989.

PECK, JOHANNE T., GINNY MCCAIG, and MARY ELLEN SAPP. *Kindergarten Policies: What Is Best for Children?* Washington, D.C: Research Monographs of National Association for the Education of Young Children, Vol. 2, 1988.

ROBINSON, JACQUELINE. *The Baby Boards: A Parents' Guide to Preschool and Primary School Entrance Tests.* New York: ARCO, 1988.

WILKES, PAUL. "The First Test of Childhood." *Newsweek* 114 (August 14, 1989): 8.

WINN, MARIE. *Children Without Childhood.* New York: Penguin, 1983.

ZIGLER, EDWARD F. "Formal Schooling for Four-Year-Olds? No." In *Early Schooling: The National Debate,* edited by Sharon L. Kagan and Edward F. Zigler. New Haven: Yale University Press, 1987.

Picture-Story Books for Pre-Kindergarteners and Kindergarteners

If you can't locate these books in your bookstore, you may be able to find many of them at your local public library.

COHEN, MIRIAM. *First Grade Takes a Test.* Illustrations by Lillian Hoban. New York: Greenwillow Books, 1980.

_____. *No Good in Art.* Illustrations by Lillian Hoban. New York: Greenwillow Books, 1980.

_____. *See You Tomorrow, Charles.* Illustrations by Lillian Hoban. New York: Greenwillow Books, 1983.

_____. *When Will I Read?* Illustrated by Lillian Hoban. New York: Greenwillow Books, 1977.

_____. *Will I Have a Friend?* Illustrations by Lillian Hoban. New York: Macmillan, 1967.

CREWS, DONALD. *School Bus.* New York, Greenwillow Books, 1984.

HAMILTON-MERRIT, JANE. *My First Days of School.* New York: Simon and Schuster, Inc., 1982.

HOWE, JAMES. *When You Go to Kindergarten.* Photographs by Betsy Imershein. New York: Alfred A. Knopf, Inc., 1986.

SCARRY, RICHARD. *Richard Scarry's Great Big Schoolhouse.* New York: Random House, 1979.

SCHWARTZ, AMY. *Annabelle Swift, Kindergartener.* New York: Frank-
lin Watts, 1988.
WELLS, ROSEMARY. *Timothy Goes to School.* New York: Dial Press,
1981.

Index